THE
WINES OF
THE RHÔNE

Regional Guides to the Wines of France

THE
WINES OF
THE RHÔNE

ARABELLA WOODROW

Series Editor: Simon Loftus

HAMLYN

Half title page picture
*This type of machinery is no longer used
but is attractive to see.*

Title page picture
*The chapel of St Christopher keeps its vigil
over the busy town of Tain l'Hermitage.*

First published in 1990
by the Hamlyn Publishing Group Limited
a division of the Octopus Publishing Group
Michelin House
81 Fulham Road
London SW3 6RB

Text © Arabella Woodrow 1989
Foreword © Simon Loftus 1989
Illustrations © The Hamlyn
Publishing Group Limited 1989

ISBN 0 600 56748 6

Produced by Mandarin Offset – printed in Hong Kong

CONTENTS

FOREWORD

The Rhône is perhaps the oldest wine growing region of France and guards its traditions well. Some of its most important grape varieties were brought there by traders from Persia in classical times, and the pattern of terraces on the steep slopes of Côte Rôtie and Hermitage may well have been established by the Romans. More important for the modern wine drinker, the Rhône remains a land of sturdy individuals, small growers making some of the world's finest wines in tiny cellars with floors of beaten earth. You may still see horses ploughing between the vines in the more accessible vineyards, while the high terraces are cultivated entirely by hand. And the best wines are hand-bottled, straight from the cask, without fining or filtration.

Despite the appalling industrial pollution which poisons the atmosphere and ruins the landscape immediately south of Lyons, despite vast hydro electric schemes and clusters of nuclear power stations, the Rhône remains a region of great tranquility, enormously resistant to change. The rhythms of country life have a reassuring timelessness: nowhere in France pays a greater homage to the ritual of the two-hour lunch.

I was rash enough to call on Auguste Clape, grower of Cornas, at ten minutes before midday. His wife greeted me at the door, her hands dripping red. For a moment I thought of murder, then realized it was the stain of blackcurrants. Monsieur Clape himself emerged from his kitchen garden across the road, clutching a bunch of radishes. There was no question of tasting the new vintage at such a moment – I hastily rearranged my appointment for the afternoon. 'Bon Appetit' they said cheerfully, and closed the door.

On another day, at about the same time, I stopped to ask directions from a curious character, the only person visible on the streets of Tournon. He tried to sell me a brown paper bag full of enormous snails and then pointed out my direction with an air of disbelief that anyone should ignore the imperatives of the hour. 'Bon Appetit', he muttered reprovingly.

A healthy appetite is indeed essential, for the Rhône produces full-flavoured wines of strong character, intended to be enjoyed with food. Hardly a bottle conforms to the anaemic, ingratiating blandness of the mass market. Curiously enough, these sunfilled southern wines are perfect with winter fare. The reds are delicious with game or with English classics like steak and kidney pudding and the whites are enhanced by a heartwarming dish of *quenelles de brochet*. Even sparkling St Péray, the Rhône's nearest equivalent to champagne is not really an aperitif wine: it has an earthy vigour which goes splendidly with *andouillettes* .

Understanding the grape varieties is relatively straightforward. Reds of the northern Rhône are made from the spicy Syrah, which smells of vanilla when young and gains an autumnal smokiness with age. At first sight the south seems more complex — Châteauneuf can be made from as many as thirteen different grapes — but in practice things are fairly simple. Southern reds come principally from Grenache (the region's workhorse, occasionally capable of great things), Mourvèdre (a wonderful grape with a bitter-rich depth of flavour) and Syrah, the northern classic. White Rhônes are either a mixture of Marsanne and Roussanne (blackthorn and limeblossom) or un-blended Viognier, that lovely rarity which has the scent of fresh apricots.

Much more effort and exploration is needed to learn about the producers and it is here that you will find this book particularly helpful. Arabella Woodrow has wide-ranging, first-hand experience of the region and pro-vides a reliable, topical guide to who is currently making the best wines in each appellation. Such a guide can never be definitive because the situation is constantly changing. A new generation is taking over, encouraged by in-creasing recognition (and better prices) for wines of real quality. Fathers who might have worried, a decade ago, that their cherished traditions were on the point of extinction now find themselves both supported and chal-lenged by sons who respect that heritage but are anxious to apply the lessons learnt at the wine school of Montpellier and from producers in other regions, even from overseas: a startling modification of the regional chau-vinism which has inhibited developments in the past. On every visit I dis-cover wonderful wines, from cellars which had not previously been worth visiting.

So there may be names missing from these pages which will soon be famous, but I applaud Arabella's bold attempt at a listing of the best pro-ducers and I have much enjoyed reading her clear and informative sum-mary of the characteristics of each village and appellation.

I hope, finally, that this book encourages you to visit the region. Enjoying the wines of the Rhône at home with friends is a tremendous plea-sure, especially when the weather is cold or wet, but nothing beats a leisurely exploration of the vineyards and the cellars, a climb up the terraces above Côte Rôtie, a drive up the foothills of the Dentelles de Montmirail and a leisurely lunch in a peaceful local restaurant. And afterwards, as the sun sparkles off the river, you may recall the ancient song, and dance on the bridge of Avignon.

© SIMON LOFTUS 1989

THE
RHÔNE VALLEY
AND ITS WINES

*It is virtually impossible to see the earth under the big stones
in this vineyard in Châteauneuf-du-Pape.*

INTRODUCTION

The Rhône river begins its life in a Swiss glacier, flowing clean and cold into France, west of Geneva. Five hundred miles later it emerges into the warm Mediterranean near Marseille. So say the geography books, though they may often neglect to mention the beautiful countryside and fabulous wines that can be found in between.

Not all of the valley has vineyards; only the part between Vienne, south of Lyon, continuing through Valence, Bollène, Orange and Avignon, as the river flows seawards. Physically, the vineyards can be divided into two parts: the northern section from Vienne to Valence, and the much larger southern part from Bollène to Avignon which also spreads to the east and west of the river valley.

Many travellers never get nearer to the region than the A7 autoroute linking Lyon to the Côte d'Azur or the roads to Spain. However, for historian, gastronome, sightseer and wine-lover alike there is enough to explore in the Rhône valley to justify spending a whole holiday there. Food is as good a reason as any; good eating leads the way to trying fine wine. While gastronomy is an integral part of French life anywhere, the fertile Rhône valley can offer a multitude of specialities. Orchards line the path of the river in the northern section, producing an abundance of pears, peaches, apricots and cherries (try the delicious locally made jams and fruit tarts). Artichokes and asparagus are especially good in season too.

In the hotter South, lavender and herbs prevail. Basil and marjoram are cultivated near St Rémy and tarragon on the Vaucluse plateau, while thyme, rosemary and savory grow wild on the hillsides across the whole southern area. Olive groves are a common sight around Nyons; garlic and olive oil feature strongly in local recipes. According to an old Provençal saying, 'A fish lives in water and dies in olive oil.'

Poultry and game thrive in the countryside and hills along the whole length of the river. An excellent variety of cow and goat's cheeses is also made. To finish off a meal, there is the famous nougat of Montélimar (reputed to have the stickiest door handles in the south of France!), made from locally grown almonds.

Top-notch provender encourages top-class restaurants, with which the Rhône valley is richly endowed. A true gourmet can relish a Michelin 3-star meal at the Restaurant Pic in Valence and try the splendid northern wines: red or white Hermitage, red Cornas or Côte Rôtie, perhaps with *foie de canard au marc d'Hermitage*. There is another fine meal to be had in the south at L'Oustau Baumanière, at Les Baux en Provence, this time with Gigondas or Châteauneuf-du-Pape. After lunch at this or one of the other good restaurants in Les Baux, stroll through the ancient village and visit its castle and medieval buildings.

The region offers sights of great historical interest, most of which date back to Roman times or even earlier. A holiday spent exploring these places and enjoying the local wine and food can be immensely satisfying and can be achieved at a leisurely, peaceful pace.

The northern vineyard area really starts south of Vienne, a city of Roman origin where there is much to see: chief among the many historic buildings is the Cathédrale St Maurice with Roman and Gothic architecture. Most of the well-known vineyards lie on the west side of the river but at Tain l'Hermitage the vines are planted on the east bank. A long climb up a narrow winding road on the hill of Hermitage affords an excellent view. Here is a chapel dedicated to St Christopher, built by the holy knight Gaspard de Stérimberg. On his return from the Crusades he was captivated by the view from the hill and Blanche of Castile, Queen of France at the time, granted him permission to build a retreat. He lived there for thirty years till his death, devoting his solitary life to the cultivation of grapes. It now gives its name to one of the most sought-after wines in this area, Paul Jaboulet's Hermitage La Chapelle.

In the southern part of the Rhône valley, the influence of Roman culture is very evident. A delightful day can start at Orange, visiting the most beautiful and best preserved Roman theatre in existence. At Vaison-la-Romaine the traffic is much less, so you can view in peace the splendid ruins, including a theatre, the Roman river bridge in the upper part of the town and the cloisters of the Notre Dame Cathedral. By now it will be time for lunch; why not have yours

GIGOT D'AGNEAU FARCI EN CROUTE

1 kg (2 lb) leg of spring lamb, boned
a little unsalted butter, softened
350 g (12 oz) puff pastry
1 egg yolk

For the stuffing
6 lamb's kidneys, diced
2 tbls unsalted butter, melted
a few sprigs of dried thyme, rosemary and tarragon,
*   crumbled*
100 g (4 oz) mushrooms, finely chopped
75 g (3 oz) truffles, chopped
50 ml (2 fl oz) Madeira
salt and pepper

Get the butcher to bone the lamb if you do not feel you can do it yourself.

To prepare the stuffing, stew the diced kidneys very gently in the melted butter for a minute or so over a moderate heat. Then add the herbs, chopped mushrooms, truffles, Madeira and seasoning. Leave to cool before stuffing the cavity in the leg of lamb. Sew up the cavity with a trussing needle.

To cook, preheat the oven to 200°C/400°F/Gas Mark 6. Rub the meat with a little softened butter and place in an ovenproof dish. Cook in the oven for 15 minutes until the meat browns on the outside. Remove and allow to cool. Reduce the oven temperature to 180°C/350°F/Gas Mark 4.

Roll out the pastry and wrap around the cooled meat then place on a baking sheet. Glaze with the egg yolk, beaten up with two drops of water. Make a criss-cross pattern with a knife point on the pastry. Bake for 15–20 minutes in the oven when the meat should be sufficiently cooked and the pastry golden brown.

Recipe from *L'Oustau de Baumanière*, Les Baux de Provence (Bouches du Rhône) adapted from Secrets of the Great French Restaurants, Louisette Bertholle.

---

with a glass or two of wine in one of the cafés bordering the market square? Or drive on up to the hillside village of Séguret, to have *truffes en chemise* at the splendid La Table du Comtat. The view from here is stunning; on a clear day you can see for miles around.

Cultural sights nestle in the rocky landscape, the *garrigues*, of the Gard *département*. The most famous of these must be the Pont du Gard near the town of Remoulins. This three-layered aqueduct over the river Gard was built by the Romans to carry water from Uzès to Nîmes. The Pont du Gard alone merits a special journey, but there is more to do here besides. For example, you can hire a canoe to see the Pont du Gard from the river or to explore the Gardon Gorges. Naturally there will be opportunities to sample the local fare at, say, Le Vieux Castillon in Castillon du Gard. Here you can compare the Gard wines with those from the Drôme or Vaucluse, with maybe a *filet de lapereau aux olives*.

While in the Gard, you should visit the Roman towns of Arles and Nîmes. Arles hosts bullfights in its amphitheatre, and concerts and plays in the Roman theatre. The Romanesque St Trophime Cloisters and the museums of Christian Art and Pagan Art must also be seen. Nîmes is not far away; allow an hour or two to visit the famous Roman monuments, especially the well-preserved amphitheatre in the city centre.

Avignon is at the centre of the southern Rhône vineyards. Immortalized by its incomplete bridge over the river, its claim to fame is as the City of the Popes. The Palace of the Popes, built in the time of Benedict XII, is a magnificent example of architecture. The Pope's summer palace at Châteauneuf-du-Pape is now in ruins, but this is the heart of the wine country. You can taste wine in many cellars in this town and can also visit Père Anselme's wine museum.

The Rhône valley may be rich in historical and epicurean delights but it is still the home of modern industry. The flowing river, swollen on its journey south by the Ouvèze, Drôme, Ardèche and Durance, among others, is naturally suitable for hydroelectric projects which have brought both wealth and skilled labour to the region. The dam at Donzère-Mondragon is deemed to be responsible for a permanent alteration to the weather; the ferocious mistral wind blows less predictably since it was built. Other heavy industries include the atomic energy base near Chusclan and the metallurgical factories near Vienne. This industrial proliferation has, however, robbed vineyard owners of much of their skilled labour. A well-paid job in a local factory is a more attractive proposition than tough manual work on steep, rocky hillsides, often for less money. As a result, the area planted with vines in many vineyards between Vienne and Valence has been reduced in recent years.

Nevertheless, the splendid wines of the Rhône continue to exert a powerful influence on the everyday life of the region. Enter any town or village at midday and the only sign of activity will be concerned with serving food and drink. Make the most of this important daily rite, the two-hour lunch break, and enjoy your meal with a bottle of the local wine.

THE RHÔNE VALLEY REGION

The part of the Rhône valley that is now planted with vineyards has seen a host of foreign tribes who settled there over hundreds of years from before the dawn of civilization to the present day. Although history records visits from Ligurian savages, Celtic farmers and Phoenician traders, it was not until 600 BC that vines were first known to have been planted, courtesy of Phocaean Greeks from Asia Minor. They also founded Marseille. Although no longer a wine capital, it is believed to be France's oldest city.

The Phocaean colony prospered, but was then overrun by Persians, bringing with them the Syrah vine variety that dominates red wine production in the northern Rhône vineyards today. Syrah is named after Shiraz, the capital of the state of Fars in Iran.

Civilization developed apace with the advent of the Romans, responsible for the foundation of such beautiful cities as Nîmes, Orange, Vienne and Vaison-la-Romaine. The Romans extended viticulture throughout the Rhône valley and onwards to the rest of France.

The wine of the Romans bore little resemblance to what we have today. Resin was added as a preservative. In time Vienne became famous for its *vinum picatum*, sufficiently prized to be re-exported to Rome. The Romans also built stone terraces in the vineyards by hand; on the steep slopes their structure still remains today.

After the fall of Rome, the wine trade went into the doldrums for a few hundred years until the Church emerged as a major owner of vineyards in the 9th century. Wines were regarded as a source of income, rather than merely an adjunct to church services.

In the thirteenth century the Popes came to Avignon from Rome. Pope Clement V planted some vines there and built a new papal palace. His successor, John XXII, constructed another, an enormous summer residence above the village ten miles north of Avignon on the foundations of a nearby ruin. This was the Pope's new castle, or Châteauneuf-du-Pape. It now lies in ruins, bombed by the Germans in the Second World War, but gave its name to the town that now sits below it, and to the Rhône valley's best known wine.

In the north, Hermitage became famous. Early in the nineteenth century its red wines were the most expensive in France, dearer than first-growth claret. The latter was often strengthened with Hermitage wine, to give a highly prized result. Nathaniel Johnston wrote of the quality of Lafitte [sic] 1795 that 'made up with Hermitage it was the best liked wine of any of that year'. This practice was at its peak in the 1860s where labels such as Margaux-Hermitage could be found, which surely must have made a mockery of the then newly introduced 1855 classification of the wines of the Médoc.

The naming of wines up until the early eighteenth century was haphazard, but was usually based on the name of the nearest town, the vineyard or its owner. In England, early Rhône imports bore names such as Vin d'Avignon (probably a Châteauneuf), Vin de la Nerte (also a Châteauneuf) or Vin de Mure – a merchant in Tain l'Hermitage whose wine was probably Crozes-Hermitage.

The year 1731 saw the first official grouping of village names. Several villages in the Gard *département*, including Tavel, Chusclan and Orsan, could use the generic title 'Côtes du Rhône'. Participating communities advertised their membership by branding the letters CdR on their wine barrels. The Drôme and Vaucluse *départements* now also produce Côtes du Rhône.

Viticulture was severely threatened in the late nineteenth century by the advent of the phylloxera louse. It came from America to Lirac, in the Gard, attacking vine roots, sucking out the sap and eventually killing the plants. Drastic cures were attempted, from flooding vineyards to electrocuting the soil. The pests survived, but are now kept at bay by grafting vines on to resistant American rootstocks.

Over two centuries ago wine communities recognized the need to protect their wines from adulteration and maintain standards of quality. However, no controlling rules were instigated until as late as 1923. The first laws were established by Baron Le Roy, the leader of the growers in Châteauneuf-du-Pape. These were the precursors of the *appellation contrôlée* laws in force today, and earned Baron Le Roy the unusual distinction of having his statue erected during his own lifetime.

By 1936 the fundamental principles of these rules had been applied to all the great vineyard areas of

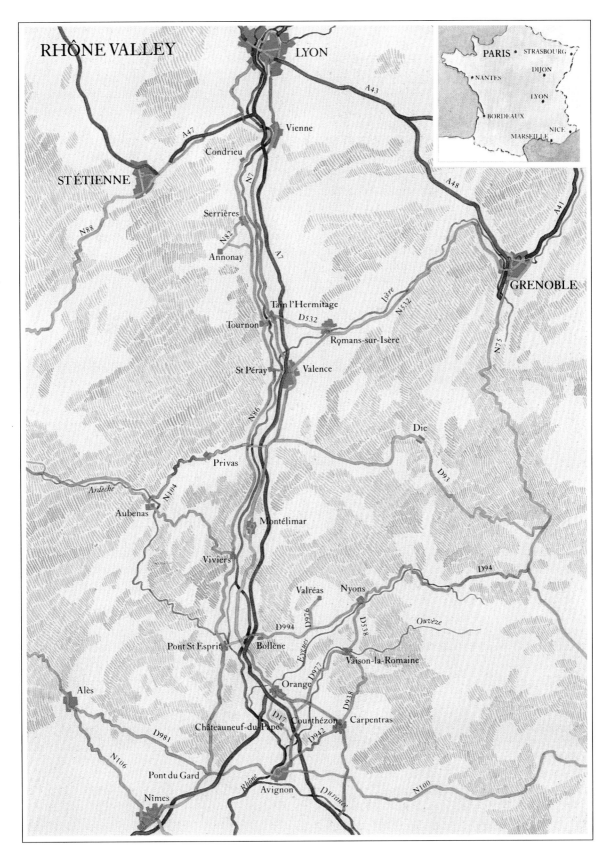

France. The best quality wines were necessarily subject to the most restrictions, while the lesser wines were less rigidly controlled. The better known names, such as Côte Rôtie, Cornas, Condrieu, Hermitage and Châteauneuf-du-Pape were all established as of *appellation contrôlée* status in 1936. Other names took longer to be acknowledged worthy of this status; Gigondas, for example, did not achieve this until 1971.

The vineyards of the Rhône valley appellations conveniently lie in almost a straight line on either side of the river. In the northern section, the slopes are so steep that the road and rail networks also follow the river, making a tour of the appellations relatively simple. Further south the terrain is flatter and the vineyards occupy a much larger area. In between the two parts is a journey of about 50 km/30 miles that at present passes no *appellation contrôlée* vineyards. Montélimar and its nougat dominate this part.

A tour of the region could well start from Lyon. As the A7 autoroute heading south approaches Vienne, the built-up industrial area subsides in favour of more attractive scenery. Leave the motorway at the Ampuis exit and take the N86 south. Here the valley is at its narrowest. The Côte Rôtie slopes rise steeply above the road as it leads towards the white wine enclave of Condrieu. Here is also found Château Grillet, the Rhône valley's smallest appellation. You may be able to buy Condrieu in the town, but as two-thirds of Château Grillet's production goes to the excellent, 2-star Michelin Hotel Beau Rivage, you may have difficulty finding this wine anywhere else. However, this is a good place to stop for lunch and try some wines while planning the onward journey.

Twenty-five km/15 miles south of Vienne begin the vineyards of St-Joseph, a source of good wines, both red and white. These lie on the slopes rising from the west bank of the river, extending just south of Tournon. Across the river is Tournon's sister town, Tain l'Hermitage. Behind Tain lies an even steeper hill, where the legendary vineyards of Hermitage are planted.

'The sun sets last on the hill of Hermitage.' Have tea or a drink in Tournon and you will observe the truth of this saying. This is part of the reason why Hermitage wines can be so good. Both Hermitage and Crozes-Hermitage owe their fortune to red wines, but each makes creditable whites as well.

Before the main roads from Tain and Tournon converge on the city of Valence are the small, peaceful villages of Cornas and St-Péray, which comprise the last of the northern appellations. Both are on the western bank of the river. Cornas produces a sturdy red wine but white wine is made at St-Péray, whose vineyards run from the Ardèchois hills down to the plain towards Valence. St-Péray is also the home of sparkling wine, but a little still white wine is also made.

The southern Rhône vineyards start with the Coteaux du Tricastin. Travelling towards Donzère, the steep hills, orchards and deciduous trees give way to olive groves, lavender fields, rocky outcrops and herbal scrub. Here the inescapable mistral wind brings clear skies and an air of the Mediterranean: there is no doubt that you are, at last, really in the South of France.

The next landmark is Orange, central to the large area, spanning three *départements*, which comprises the vineyards of the Côtes du Rhône. To see the best of this region, a number of side excursions from a single base is recommended – though possibly not from Orange for, while its architecture is splendid, the noise and traffic are dreadful. A quiet hotel in a nearby village is a better idea.

Here you will be treated to a wide variety of scenery and soils. In the Gard, to the west of the river, the landscape is bare and rocky, with the highest ground near Tavel, which produces only rosé wine, and Lirac, which makes red and white as well. By contrast, the Vaucluse vineyards near the villages of Vacqueyras, Sablet, Séguret and Cairanne are on gentler slopes of sand, clay and stones. On a clear day there is a panoramic view from Sablet for miles around. The neighbouring village, Gigondas, has its vineyards on higher slopes leading up to the Dentelles de Montmirail, the spiky, tooth-shaped rock formation on the mountains presiding over the Plan de Dieu to the west.

Back towards the main N7 between Orange and Avignon, turn off at Courthezon to reach Châteauneuf-du-Pape, along tiny roads. The ruins of the castle can be seen at a distance, perched on a hill overlooking the town. Vineyards lie all around on gently undulating slopes. Many are covered with large cream- and rust-coloured stones, which act as storage heaters to retain and radiate the heat of the sun, ripening the grapes of Châteauneuf to produce some of the fullest bodied wines, red and white, in all of France.

South of Avignon the landscape changes to the sandy flats surrounding the Rhône delta. Vineyards give way to the marshes of the Camargue, which is famous for horses rather than its wine.

These vineyards at Beaumes de Venise are baked dry by the sun.
Whilst other vegetation is sparse, the vines thrive in this arid heat.

VITICULTURE –
GROWING THE GRAPES

Good quality wines in the Rhône valley are plentiful and vary widely in style. There are numerous vineyard sites of differing soil types; also a large selection of grape varieties, mostly introduced by the Romans.

Weather conditions in the Rhône valley differ as much between north and south as factors of geography and geology. The northern sector from Lyon to Valence is already sufficiently far south to enjoy warm springs and hot summers. With the hillsides of Côte Rôtie and Hermitage perfectly aligned towards the south-east and south-west respectively, vineyards receive the sun from dawn to dusk. Extra heat is also generated in the vineyards through the enclosing effect of the terrace walls. Rainfall is most likely to occur in the spring when it can hinder the flowering. Rain can also occur in the autumn when, if the weather breaks too early, it can spoil the vintage. Frost is occasionally a hazard, though by no means on the scale experienced in northern France. In the summer hailstorms are a threat; difficult to forecast, and virtually impossible to prevent, they can destroy a vineyard within minutes.

The southern part of the Rhône valley from Donzère to Avignon enjoys a distinctly Mediterranean climate, dominated by the mistral wind which blows from the mountains in the north-west. This wind dictates the lives of the southern Rhône and Provençal communities, blowing for 300 days a year and usually in multiples of three days at a time. No unlatched door or window is safe from this cold, drying wind which has been known to overturn cars on the highway. Ancient law stipulated that murder was no longer necessarily a capital crime if committed when the mistral had been blowing continuously for nine days or more. The wind is, however, beneficial to the vines as it brings clear, dry weather and prevents pests and insects from making a permanent home in the vineyards. Most vines in the southern Rhône valley have a north–south inclination resulting from years of battering from the wind. Cypress trees and canes are planted to break its force.

Rainfall is irregular, varying from non-existent to torrential, usually over short periods. The rainy periods occur in early spring and late autumn, while the summer weather is clear, dry and stable. The winters are comparatively warm with clear blue skies and apple trees blossoming as early as February in many years. Rain is often accompanied by the warm sirocco wind from the south. In late summer or autumn this combination of conditions can provide a perfect opportunity for rot or fungal disease to set in.

Since in neither part of the valley is the climate restrictive to the growth of vines, one may wonder why they are not planted everywhere, particularly in the gap between the two regions. First, one has to consider the position, or aspect, of a potential vineyard. 'Vines love an open hill' according to Virgil, who succinctly summarized several of the important principles of viticulture. Too close to sea or river level, the land may be so flat that it allows pockets of cool air to collect, bringing the risk of fog or spring frosts, and will not afford sufficient drainage. Too high up and the average temperature may not be high enough to support satisfactory growth and ripening of the grapes.

Drainage is of supreme importance; vines do not tolerate 'having wet feet' (hence the importance of Virgil's hill). Good drainage depends on the angle of the slope and the nature of the soil; better still, the hill should have a south-east or south-west aspect in order to maximize exposure to the sunshine. Hillside vineyards are less at risk from fog or frost than those on the flat as the circulation of air is better, a factor which also reduces the risk of rot and disease.

The most successful soils in the northern Rhône have a subsoil of granite; this hard rock permits excellent drainage and encourages the vine roots to dig deep into the soil. This rock formation was part of the Massif Central mountain range that lies to the west of Tournon. The Hermitage hill, on the eastern side of the river, was once part of this range until, at some stage thousands of years ago, the river changed its course to run past the western side of the hill. The rock base is covered with a fine topsoil varying from flint and chalk in Hermitage to limestone in Côte Rôtie and decomposed mica in Condrieu. In all cases this light topsoil is eroded by heavy rain and needs to be carried back up the slopes and repacked down every year; this is a backbreaking, labour-intensive task that must have contributed to the abandonment of some of the steeper slopes.

A vineyard in winter can be bleak and cold,
though work on the vines must still go on. Burning the vine
prunings helps relieve the cold and clears the ground.

Erosion is less of a force to be reckoned with in the flatter vineyards of the southern Rhône; here the soils are more varied. In Châteauneuf-du-Pape retreating Alpine glaciers from the Pliocene era left large rounded quartz stones and boulders over a subsoil of red, iron-rich, sand, clay and limestone base. This soil is almost perfect for cultivating vines as the top-soil and subsoil afford excellent drainage, assisted by the drying mistral. This reduces the quantity of grapes yielded but enormously improves the quality, further assisted by the large stones which absorb the heat of the sun by day and radiate warmth at night. Vineyard workers hate these stones as they cause un-told damage to machinery but they do provide an im-measurable boost to the quality and alcoholic degree of the wine.

Elsewhere in the vineyards of the southern Rhône valley, soils are varied and consist of a combination of clay, sand, limestone, gravel, stones and the rocky *garrigues*. The best sites are on the gentle slopes that provide good drainage such as the Gigondas vineyards in the foothills of the Dentelles de Mont-mirail, the chalky slopes of Tavel and the gentle hills on clay leading to the villages of Sablet and Rasteau.

In the Rhône valley, as elsewhere, different soil structures are suited to different grape varieties. Minor soil variations throughout the valley's vineyard area allow many grape varieties to be planted, particularly in the south; unlike in Cham-pagne or Burgundy where the particular combina-tion of soil and climate only permit successful culti-vation of the Pinot family of grapes. For example, Châteauneuf-du-Pape can be produced by a com-bination of up to thirteen different grape varieties. Though few producers use them all, most believe that even the minor ones have a contribution to make which justifies their inclusion in the vineyard.

Red and white grapes both thrive throughout the Rhône valley, though it is rare to find a site that supports both equally well. The main grape variety in the northern vineyards is the red Syrah, which lends itself well to the hard granitic rock and enjoys the warm Mediterranean climate of the Rhône valley. It does not thrive in cooler, wetter regions such as Burgundy, Bordeaux or the Loire valley, though it is also planted successfully in the hotter vineyards of Australia and South Africa, where it is commonly known as Shiraz.

Syrah is the only red grape variety permitted in the northern part of the Rhône valley. It is also grown in parts of the southern area to contribute vinosity, colour, flavour and tannin to the wines. But in the south the red Grenache grape predominates. In hot climates the Grenache can give wines of enormous alcoholic degree, up to 14 degrees alcohol, with plenty of vigour and vinosity. It does not thrive in cooler, slightly wetter areas as it is sensitive to cold weather at flowering time. For this reason it is not permitted in the northern sector.

In Châteauneuf-du-Pape, six red grape varieties are permitted besides Syrah and Grenache (the other five being white). Outside Châteauneuf the main plantings are of Grenache, supplemented by Syrah, Cinsault and Mourvèdre according to the soil type and the whims of the vineyard owner. The ignoble Carignan grape (widely planted in Provence and the Midi giving large quantities of often indifferent wine) can occasionally be found though its use is being discouraged in Côtes du Rhône.

Many white grape varieties are planted in the southern vineyards: Grenache Blanc is the main one for white Côtes du Rhône. However, it is not one of the five white varieties allowed in Châteauneuf-du-Pape.

The white Roussanne, allowed in Châteauneuf, and another white variety, the Marsanne (permitted in white Côtes du Rhône but not Châteauneuf), are also grown in the northern sector of the Rhône valley. In St-Péray, some of the white grapes are known as Roussette, though these are believed to be identical to Roussanne. In theory, St-Péray may be made from Marsanne, Roussanne and Roussette. French fraud inspectors reckon that Roussette should be excluded but cannot identify it!

There is another white grape variety grown in the northern sector that is extremely rare and difficult to cultivate: the Viognier. It is planted on the hills of Condrieu and in the tiny vineyard of Château Grillet, below the village of St-Michel-sur-Rhône. In these areas, the granite has a topsoil of decomposed mica, which can support the Viognier. It is little cultivated elsewhere and, indeed, is capricious and unpredictable even where it does grow. Sometimes the grapes do not ripen properly, for no apparent reason; yields are always small but the vine can achieve great longevity. The rewards come in a good year when wines of infinite subtlety, finesse and delicacy are produced: these need time to mature but repay it handsomely.

The success of the Viognier, or any other grape variety, is strongly influenced by the amount it is allowed to yield, which in turn can be controlled by the methods of cultivation. A vine needs to be trained by a method that permits ease of cultivation and harvesting; at the same time it needs to be pruned in order to restrict the growth of foliage at the expense of fruit, and to control the overall crop of fruit to make the most of qualities offered by the soil. The *appellation contrôlée* laws stipulate the maximum permitted yields; the better the quality of the wine, the lower the yield can be. Thus Côte Rôtie and Condrieu are permitted to make only 35 and 30 hectolitres per hectare respectively, at most, while generic Côtes du Rhône can be made from yields of 50. Confusingly, these permitted yields can be altered each year according to the conditions, so that a potentially large crop of good quality need not be sacrificed. In addition, a tolerance of 20 per cent is allowed over the so-called maximum so the yield should never be overly restrictive.

The Syrah grape is trained on wires in the southern Côtes du Rhône vineyards to allow air to circulate to minimize the effect of rot. All other grape varieties in the southern part are cultivated low in the *gobelet* or bush shape, low down in order to benefit from the heat radiated from the stony ground. This, however, is changing with the advent of mechanical harvesting; machine pickers need to have the grapes carefully oriented in order to collect them efficiently and economically. Because *gobelet* training cannot offer this, many vines are now being trained on wires, *à la guyot*, instead.

Neither mechanical harvesting nor even training on wires is practical on the steep slopes further north. All picking must be done by hand, and only the sensitive Viognier is trained *guyot*-style. Syrah, Marsanne and Roussanne grapes are trained *en gobelet*; in the Côte Rôtie vineyards, however, the slopes are so steep that the vines have to be supported in groups on stakes, known as the *taille Côte Rôtie*.

SYRAH   GRENACHE   VIOGNIER

THE MAIN RED GRAPE VARIETIES

Syrah Syrah is a hardy variety that thrives in hot climates on well-exposed sites, preferably with stony or granitic soils. The grapes grow in medium-sized bunches with small, oval, purple-violet berries. The smallness of the berries and their thick skins, combined with the fact that this vine rarely yields more than 30 hectolitres per hectare allows it to produce highly coloured wines, concentrated in bouquet, flavour and tannin. The thick skins protect the grapes from most diseases, though the vine can be subject to *coulure* if bad weather persists at flowering time. The characteristic fruit flavour of Syrah is that of smoky blackcurrants or blackberries when young, and of violets and spice when the wine is older, together with a spicy, rich cedarwood smokiness. The wines are also high in tannin, extract and acid allowing them to age well.

Grenache Grenache comes from Spain, where it is known as Garnacha. It grows well on dry, stony ground and thrives on the large stones of Châteauneuf-du-Pape. It is best suited to warm or hot climates as it ripens late and is susceptible to spring frosts and bad weather at flowering. Unlike the Syrah it is comparatively thin-skinned and is, therefore, more sensitive to rot in rainy conditions, though this is not usually a major hazard in the Rhône valley. Grenache wines are relatively pale in colour unless the yield is strictly curtailed in which case darker, more concentrated wines can be made. It produces highly alcoholic wines, as much as 15

degrees in some years, with a sweet raspberry fruit and herby character. They contain little tannin but their full body contributes vinosity and solidity to the wines.

Cinsault Cinsault produces a full-coloured, soft, medium-bodied wine that is low in tannin, high in fruit and contributes finesse and softness to a blend, although it lacks sufficient character to be used by itself.

Mourvèdre Mourvèdre succeeds in warm areas and does best planted on slopes with comparatively rich soils, where it can give deep-coloured wine with plenty of tannin and body and a spicy, bitter character to the aroma.

THE MAIN WHITE GRAPE VARIETIES

Viognier This variety is peculiarly difficult to cultivate successfully and is, therefore, seldom found outside the Rhône valley. It has small berries and gives a low yield of wine with a rich, complex, apricot flavour and an earthy taste, a *goût de terroir*. The wine can oxidize rapidly, but if care is taken in making it, this maderization is not necessarily unpleasant.

If the weather is bad it is difficult to grow Viognier and sometimes the crop fails even if the weather is favourable. The average yield is very small, just 16 hectolitres per hectare, but the vine has the potential for long life – fifty to seventy years – though its prime age for bearing fruit is between thirty and fifty years of age.

Marsanne Marsanne is rarely grown without its partner Roussanne nearby. It is the sturdier and higher yielding of the two, though its wine has less acidity and finesse.

Roussanne Roussanne is considered to be more noble than Marsanne, and the wines produced have aromas which have been likened to nuts, coffee, honey and flowers.

THE VINEYARD YEAR

Each year there is a continuous cycle of jobs to do in the vineyard in order to grow grapes successfully. After each vintage the vineyard needs to be cleared of dead leaves. Dead vines must be uprooted. In the winter months the dedication of the *vigneron*, the man who grows the vines, will be most tested: in the cold and the rain or snow, the tedious jobs of re-placing posts and wires and pruning last year's dead wood from the vine all need to be done.

Pruning lasts from December to February; although, if February turns out mild, it is wise to have finished pruning earlier, as the warm weather can cause the sap to rise. Pruning after the sap has risen causes wounds which heal only with great diffi-culty. In February it is not unusual to find local restaurants offering meat grilled over *sarments*, the dead prunings, which make a delicious barbecue.

In March, new vines must be planted out and the vineyard ploughed. Buds will start to appear at this time. It is unlikely that these will suffer from frost in the Rhône valley. However, some spray the buds with sulphur in case rain brings the hazard of powdery mildew, a fungal disease that can attack the shoots or, later on, the flowers and fruit.

June is a crucial time for the *vigneron* because it is then that the critical flowering takes place. The flowers are self-pollinating and produce the berries that will become grapes. Flowering is successful in warm, dry, stable conditions; if the weather is cold or rainy the flowers cannot form properly and those plants will yield no grapes. Such a misfortune is known as *coulure*, one to which the Grenache variety is very susceptible. Obviously, the potential size of the crop can be judged after the flowering, though not its quality, as this will be determined by the weather in the last weeks preceding the harvest.

The size of the crop can be no greater than that in-dicated by the flowering; it could be a lot less if a hail-storm strikes. Nothing can be done to influence or prevent hail, just hope and insurance. The grower can, however, exert some measure of control over the ravages of pests and diseases.

The vine will be protected from the phylloxera louse by grafting the young vine on to American rootstocks before planting. Other pests, such as caterpillars, moths, red spiders and beetles, need to be repelled on a regular basis. Normally, sulphur and insecticide sprays are used. The *vigneron* has to contend also with fungal diseases though happily the mistral wind's drying effect reduces the risk of these occurring in the Rhône valley. All vineyards are likely to be sprayed with copper sulphate, sulphur and fungicides on a regular basis to make quite sure that no disease takes hold. Rot on the grapes imparts an unpleasant and easily noticeable taste to the wine.

In the period from June to August, these spraying treatments will be applied regularly. At the same time the *vigneron* will need either to spray or hoe the soil to restrict the growth of weeds.

During this time the hard, small, green berries that result from the flowering will form, and gradu-ally swell, soften and change colour into either yellow or black (for white or red varieties, respectively). No more spraying takes place after this, in order not to taint the fruit when picked; now the weather does all the work. In the last three or four weeks before pick-ing, the final ripening takes place. During this time the *vigneron* hopes for hot, dry, sunny conditions: cold now may prevent complete ripening, and rain may cause excess water to be absorbed to give a thin, dilute wine. Worse still, rain may instigate rot.

White grapes are picked in September in the Rhône valley though the Viognier is picked later than the other white varieties. Red grapes tend to be ripe for picking around the end of September.

In the northern area hand-picking is the only means possible on the steep slopes. Machine-picking is commercially feasible in vineyards on flatter ground and is seen in the larger vineyards in the Côtes du Rhône areas. In Châteauneuf-du-Pape the grapes are likely to be hand-picked; the *appellation contrôlée* laws stipulate a sorting of grapes.

The exact date of picking will influence the quality of the wine enormously: too early and the grapes will be green and overacidic. For red wines it is worth waiting to achieve full ripeness so that the wines have plenty of colour and flavour, though with white grapes it is desirable to retain sufficient acidity; in the hot Mediterranean climate it is only too easy to make a heavy, flabby wine. Sometimes it may rain during the harvest. If the rain is short-lived, it is possible to wait, hoping that subsequent sunny weather will allow the ripening to be completed.

VINIFICATION –
MAKING THE WINE

The art of making wine has been known for some 12 000 years. Early attempts to ferment grape juice to make a palatable wine were fraught with danger from infections and, mainly, the risk of oxidation – exposing the wine to the air – resulting in unpleasant, vinegary wines. Happily winemaking is now much less of a hit-and-miss affair, drawing on the experience of countless generations and benefiting from modern methods and technology.

It is certain that good wine can only come from good-quality grapes. Even then, poor vinification can fail to realize the potential of a good crop. It is crucial that the fruit of carefully tended vines be treated properly both during and after picking. Regardless of the numerous methods and variations available to make wine, good cellar hygiene is vital to prevent spoilage.

Each of the different types of wines produced in the Rhône valley requires a different method of vinification, to say nothing of the countless individual variations. It would be confusing to describe every one. What follows is an account of the general vinification process for each type of wine.

How White Wine is Made
The important factor when making white wine in a warm, southerly region such as the Rhône valley is the preservation of fruit, freshness and acidity. Early picking encourages retention of acidity but care is also needed during vinification to prevent oxidation. It is therefore vital that the grape must (fresh juice) is kept cool to keep this risk to a minimum.

White grapes will be pressed as soon as possible after picking. Grapes with leaves, earth and all will be tipped into the horizontal Vaslin presses, to emerge as a dirty brown juice. The foreign bodies must now be removed by settling or centrifugation but, as the crude must also contains the natural yeasts that formed the bloom on the grapes' skins, the fermentation process must be delayed until the settling is complete; a little sulphur dioxide will hold the yeasts at bay for the twenty-four hours needed.

Pumping the juice into fermentation vats afterwards helps dissipate the sulphur dioxide allowing the wine yeasts to start work to convert grape sugars to alcohol. To make wine that is fresh, the temperature must be controlled. It is rarely allowed to exceed 20°C/68°F if the wine is to retain its zing. Some winemakers prefer to ferment at 15–18°C/59–65°F. If the must is too cool, the wine retains all its fruit but does not develop the volatile, characteristic aromas which come from higher temperatures. Too warm and these aromas can easily become the precursors of oxidation. The modern way to ferment wine is to use vats of stainless steel. The fermenting must can be cooled in these by running cold water down the outside. This cannot be done with vats of cement or wood, which conduct heat badly. In these circumstances temperature control is normally carried out by pumping the must through a heat exchanger.

Fermentation may last anything up to ten to fourteen days. After it is finished, the dead yeasts will drop to the bottom of the vat as lees, and the wine will need to be 'racked' (transferred into a clean vessel).

Most white Rhône wines are bottled young. Château Grillet is an exception. After racking, this wine will be matured in oak barrels for a period of about eighteen months. During this time, the wine will be racked occasionally and the barrels kept topped up to prevent oxidation attacking wines in 'ullaged' vats, those in which there is any empty space.

In the maturation period two things will happen. First, in the warm spring following the vintage, another type of fermentation, known as malolactic fermentation, will take place naturally. This process slightly reduces the acidity in the wine and stabilizes it. Second, in the winter later that year, the cold will stabilize the wine further, leaving it star-bright.

White Hermitage is also made by methods similar to those for Château Grillet. Grapes are picked late to be fully ripe, giving highly alcoholic wines. They are fermented and matured in both vats and oak barrels, to be bottled some fourteen to eighteen months after the malolactic fermentation has taken place,

The more commercial white Rhône wines will not be aged in wood, but bottled in the spring following the vintage once the malolactic fermentation has occurred. Before bottling, the wine may be clarified by fining, pouring in whisked egg white, which sinks to the bottom taking with it any impurities, and filtered before bottling.

How Red Wine is Made

There is an added dimension to be considered in the production of red wines: that of colour. Red grapes grown in the Rhône valley have white juice, as is the case with virtually all varieties. The colour resides in the grape skins and can only be extracted when the skin cells are broken down, by alcohol or heat for example. The grape skins also contain the astringent tannin, so vital in young wines as a preservative. In a traditional red wine fermentation, colour and tannin are released at the same time as the alcoholic fermentation.

In the traditional method of making red wine, grapes are crushed on arrival at the cellars; the crush is first lightly sulphured and then pumped into large vats. Some winemakers prefer to remove the stalks first to obtain a less astringent wine. Since red wines require more of the volatile aromas and less of the freshness that is so important in white wines they are fermented at a higher temperature, which also helps to extract colour and tannin. Grapes are allowed to ferment at between 20° and 30°C, 68° and 86°F, though some cooling may be necessary in hot weather. The grape skins have a tendency to float on the surface of the must, propelled by the carbon dioxide gas formed during fermentation. This 'cap' or *chapeau* of skins must be regularly broken up and submerged, not only to prevent the risk of infections but also to extract as much colour and tannin as possible. Usually the wine is pumped over the cap at regular intervals.

This fermentation may take two weeks or even longer; afterwards the wine is drained off the skins. These then go back to the presses to extract the *vin de presse*, rich in colour and tannin, some or all of which can be added back to the free-run wine at the winemaker's discretion.

The wine is then matured in wooden barrels for anything from fifteen months upwards, depending on the style of the wine. During this time the barrels are racked and topped up regularly. The wine will also be clarified with gelatine or egg whites before bottling. This method will generate concentrated, highly coloured, tannic wines that may need years in bottle before they have matured sufficiently to be drinkable. This is fine for the high-quality wines that can be assured of commanding a good price, but what of the lower priced wines which may not have the concentration of fruit and flavour to withstand long ageing? Modern opinion is of the view that, while a deep colour and plenty of fruit are desirable to the consumer, astringent tannin is not. Commercial con-

siderations also lie heavily in favour of a wine that is ready to drink early on, so the wine can be sold sooner.

Since the process of alcoholic fermentation is technically separate from colour or tannin extraction, these processes can be controlled independently. As a result two different vinification methods were developed which enable the winemaker to produce red wine with greater commercial appeal.

The better known of these methods is called *macération carbonique*. Red grapes are placed whole in a closed vat containing carbon dioxide gas. Under these airless circumstances fermentation takes place inside the cells of the grape skins of the whole grapes. The grape skin cells break, releasing their colour, but not the tannin, into the must. When sufficient colour has been obtained, the vat is drained, the grapes are pressed and fermentation is allowed to proceed in the presence of air. This method permits plenty of colour to be released into the wine without it becoming hard and tannic. Wines fermented by this method will have a bright crimson colour, an appealing fruity bouquet and mature early. They will not be expected to keep for more than three to four years.

Alternatively, many growers in the south use a variation on this method called *semi-macération*. Grapes are placed whole in the vats without any carbon dioxide. A few crushed grapes may be added, but the ones at the bottom will be crushed by the weight of those at the top. Some intracellular 'maceration' fermentation will occur in the middle and some normal fermentation will occur at the top, giving essentially a combination of both methods. The wine will have plenty of fruit and colour, with some, but not too much, tannin. Growers such as M. Steinmaier at the Domaine Ste-Anne of St-Gervais (Côtes du Rhône-Villages) and M. Mejan in Lirac use this method to great effect.

Another method, called thermovinification, is based on the fact that grape skin cells can be broken down by heating which will allow the colouring pigments to escape without the tannin, which requires alcohol contact. Grapes are crushed and heated to between 70° and 90°C/158° and 194°F by passing through steam-heated pipes, to extract colour. The must is then cooled, the grapes pressed and the juice is fermented without the skins at about 20°C/68°F in the same manner as white juice would be. Very little tannin is obtained using this method, but a bright colour is produced.

These two alternative methods were pioneered in the South of France and are used extensively in the

While wines are maturing gently in oak barrels, their deposits need to be racked off regularly. The wine must also be tasted to monitor its progress.

southern part of the Rhône valley. In particular, cooperatives and *négociants* making Côtes du Rhône on a large scale use one or other of these methods to a great extent, though usually the wine made by, say, *macération carbonique* is blended with traditionally made wine in order to achieve the desired style, rather than being used on its own.

Carbonic maceration can produce wines of reasonable quality in the cheap and middle ranges, that will keep for a few years. Thermovinification is only suitable for cheaper wines, and can, even then, produce disastrous results if unskilfully applied.

HOW ROSÉ WINE IS MADE

Plenty of pink wine is produced in the Rhône valley, almost exclusively in the southern sector. It is always vinified to dryness, unlike the sweeter rosés of the Loire valley. The essence of rosé production is to give crushed red grapes a short period of maceration on their skins to allow just a little colour to seep into the must. The pink juice is then drained off and fermentation allowed to proceed as though it were a white wine. The skins may be pressed to give a much darker coloured juice which can be blended back into the wine as required. Sometimes the red grape skins have the colour extracted by an adaptation of the thermovinification method which is normally used for red wines.

Control is of vital importance. Only a little colour must be allowed to bleed into the must and the subsequent fermentation must proceed slowly under cool temperatures to retain the fruit and liveliness of the wine. In such a warm climate it follows that those with stainless steel, modern equipment have the best chance of making good rosé.

HOW SPARKLING WINE IS MADE

Sparkling wine forms a comparatively small part of the Rhône valley's vinous offerings (Clairette de Die and St-Péray, mainly). Nevertheless it requires careful vinification.

St-Péray must, by law, be made by the champagne method, even using the same strain of yeasts as the Champenoises do. To start with, the grapes are pressed and vinified as for other white wines of the region. Around April or May following the harvest the still wine is bottled with a small quantity of a blend of sugar and champagne yeasts added at the same time. Using the sugar as fuel, the yeasts begin to make alcohol once more, with carbon dioxide also being generated. This gas has no means of escape from the bottle and dissolves under the pressure to give the wine its sparkle.

The bottles are left for anything from one to four years on their sides before being stacked in wooden racks, *pupitres* for occasional very careful turning (*remuage*) to dislodge the sediment of dead yeasts towards the neck of the bottles. Then the bottles are disgorged, topped up with a solution of sugar in wine and recorked.

Clairette de Die comes in two versions: *Brut* which must be made by the champagne method and *Tradition*, which does not. The *Tradition* wine begins life as other white wines do except that the first fermentation proceeds extremely slowly by means of cooling or frequent filtrations. By the time the wine is bottled in the January following the vintage, there should still be some unfermented sugar left in the wine. No extra yeasts or sugar are added; the first fermentation simply continues inside the bottle to make the sparkle. The wine then spends at least nine months inside the bottle to complete this first fermentation, and the subsequent malolactic one. The bottles are then opened and the wine filtered under pressure and rebottled. In this way the deposits are excluded but the carbon dioxide is prevented from escaping.

HOW DESSERT WINE IS MADE

In the southern part of the Rhône valley distinctive dessert wines are produced. The village of Rasteau makes a dessert wine from the Grenache grape, while another village, Beaumes-de-Venise, produces one from Muscat, whose popularity has seen an explosive growth in recent years.

Both wines are described as *Vin Doux Naturel* or

*During the harvest, grapes are often placed in small tubs to minimize
the premature crushing of the grapes at the bottom.*

'naturally sweet wine', although they do not retain their sweetness by the force of nature alone. Both types of grape are picked late, to have as much sugar in them as possible. Fermentation is at a cool temperature so that progress is slow. When the sugar content has fallen to the desired level, grape alcohol is added to fortify the wine and prevent the wine yeasts from fermenting further. This is known as a *Vin Doux Naturel*, though wines that contain so much sugar that the fermentation stops of its own accord may be described as *Vin Naturellement Doux*: a subtle difference!

After racking, the wine may be aged in wooden vats, though this is discouraged for the Muscat wine with its fresh, spicy flavour is considered best if the wine is young.

THE PRODUCERS

The vineyards of the Rhône valley cover over 40 000 hectares/99 000 acres and range in size from about 2 hectares/5 acres (Château Grillet) to over 180 hectares/445 acres, for example Château Malijay near the village of Jonquières. Each vineyard will produce wine with its own individual style.

Demand for any wine is not conveniently fragmented into parcels the size of specific vineyards producing it but is more likely to be for a blended house style, consistent from year to year. This can only be achieved by a merchant buying up wines from a number of vineyards which he then combines to make a much larger quantity of his own blend; this is the traditional role of the *négociant*.

If a vineyard owner wishes to make and bottle his own wine, he needs to buy or borrow all the equipment required from vineyard machinery to vats to a bottling line – an expensive matter if his vineyard is small. However, he is then entitled to call his wine estate- or domaine-bottled, which has a cachet to it.

Supposing the grower does not have sufficient resources, in terms of time, money or equipment, he may dispose of his crop at an earlier stage in its production. He can sell the grapes after picking; he can press them and sell the must, or he can vinify the wine and sell it during the maturation process.

Many growers like to have long-term contracts with certain *négociants*, who undertake to buy their crop every year. To discourage complacency that crop must conform to certain pre-set criteria of quality and ripeness otherwise the buyer has the right to turn down the grapes on arrival. Other growers prefer to stake their chances on the open market. There is no reason why any grower should not vinify and bottle his best *cuvées* under the name of the estate and sell the rest to *négociants* for their house blends.

In the Rhône valley there are numerous growers. Not all may have contacts with suitable *négociants* and, conversely, a *négociant* may not know intimately which growers can produce the style of wine that he is seeking to put the finishing touches to his master blend. Therefore grower–*négociant* sales and contracts are arranged by a *courtier*, or broker, who delivers the necessary samples and quotations so that *négociants* can make their decision rapidly and efficiently. The *courtier* will not hold any stock himself but is paid a fee comprising a small percentage of the value of the sale. A number of such brokers exist in the region and their activities may include representation of growers, *négociants* and cooperatives.

The cooperative provides an alternative to the *négociant* for the grower, who may not wish to vinify all his wine himself. Cooperatives were established initially in the 1920s and 1930s to provide a central winemaking point for growers who had neither the money nor the equipment to make the wine satisfactorily themselves. They are now a regular feature throughout the South of France.

Membership of a cooperative entitles the grower to bring all his grapes to their cellars for vinification, providing his crop fulfils minimum quality standards. Each member pays a fee which goes towards the cost of installing and maintaining the equipment. In return, the cooperative will undertake to pay the grower a price, agreed before the vintage, for his grapes and look after them henceforth.

Generally, the resulting wine will not be given an estate or domaine label. Usually the wine will be blended and sold under the cooperative's own label. This may say, for example, 'Cave Coopérative de . . .' or 'Les Producteurs Réunis de . . .' under the village name or the wine's generic title, if the village name is inappropriate for that wine.

NÉGOCIANTS

Reliable *négociants* can easily be found in both sectors of the Rhône valley. Most offer a complete range of wines from both sectors, though they are more likely to specialize in the wines of the region in which they are situated. For example, Paul Jaboulet Aîné in Tain, Delas Frères outside Tournon and Guigal at Ampuis specialize in the northern region wines, while Caves Bessac in L'Isle sur la Sorgue and Caves St-Pierre in Châteauneuf are more likely to offer Châteauneuf or Gigondas.

The greatest strength of the *négociant* is his ability to offer wine that is of consistent quality, and usually follows a house style. For wines such as Côtes du Rhône it is likely that the variation between vintages will not be of any great significance. The *négociant* may also keep back some reserve wines of previous vintages so that every year he can make a non-vintage blend of better than average quality as it contains a proportion of mature wine.

The advantages of consistency may also work in the opposite direction; some excellent wines can lose their greatness and individuality in blending, although faults can be hidden by this means. It should be pointed out that some of the worst wine in the Rhône valley comes from *négociants*. Blending is a skilled job and not all merchants do it well.

Négociants are also in a position to benefit from economies of scale when it comes to purchasing equipment, hiring personnel and funding their sales activities; but, by the same token, their capital requirements are likely to be high. The cost of financing a large-scale operation in terms of initial outlay as well as the interest on expenditure is likely to be considerable, increasing the price of the wine. Included in the cost will be provisions for promoting the sales, and advertising of the wine, which should be of assistance to the professional buyer.

GROWERS

Whatever advantages the *négociant* may enjoy in terms of scale turn to disadvantages for the grower: he cannot afford to maintain or replace equipment as efficiently as the *négociant*; he may only be able to afford to install cheaper (and less effective) tanks or machines. What he can offer, however, is guaranteed individuality of style as he will only be handling wines from his own vineyards. However, the notion that the wine will be better because it has not been handled in a 'mass-production' does not always stand up to scrutiny when comparing a grower's limited facilities with a *négociant*'s modern ones.

Anyone purchasing wine from a domaine they have never tried before will enjoy the suspense of not being able to predict what lies in store. A modestly priced bottle bought at the grower's door, or perhaps a local shop or restaurant, could yield a superb wine.

Unlike the *négociants*, growers will not have a limitless supply of their wine. Once it is sold, they cannot replenish their stocks until the next year's vintage is ready. Availability is more likely to be a problem with estates producing the finer wines. In extreme cases stocks may be sold by allocation, with most potential buyers in a good year clamouring for more than their allotted share. Should you be fortunate enough to find such a wine under these circumstances, grab the opportunity when it comes. Paul Jaboulet Aîné's Hermitage La Chapelle is one of the most sought-after wines in the world and is naturally in short supply.

François Perrin owns the prestigious Château de Beaucastel estate in Châteauneuf-du-Pape.

COOPERATIVES

There are few cooperatives in the northern part of the Rhône valley. The only one of any note is the *cave coopérative* at Tain l'Hermitage. In the southern Rhône just about every wine-producing village will have its *cave coopérative*, around which the life of the whole village revolves at vintage time.

Cooperatives run on the minimum of overheads, aiming to offer wines which are fairly priced and representative of their names and appellations to a fickle market. Prices cannot afford to be high; generally a Côtes du Rhône from a cooperative will be cheaper than a top *négociant*'s offering.

While many cooperatives are still comparatively basic in terms of modern equipment, others have realized the importance of competition in today's markets. These, such as the cooperative at Villedieu-Buisson in the Vaucluse, have not only invested in up-to-date installations but also in people well-qualified to make the wine, and others to promote and sell it world-wide. Large quantities of wine are still accounted for by local consumption and passing trade. You can buy either by the bottle or by the litre in your own container, and you may also taste before you buy. This is important as the quality does vary widely between cooperatives.

LA CHAPELLE DE L'HERMITAGE

PAUL JABOULET AINÉ   PAUL JABOULET AINÉ

1986

UNION DES VIGNERONS

TAVEL

APPELLATION TAVEL CONTRÔLÉE

DE L'ENCLAVE DES PAPES

37,5cl

MIS EN BOUTEILLE PAR
LES PRODUCTEURS A.P.V.T. 30126 TAVEL
POUR LE CELLIER DE L'ENCLAVE DES PAPES A VALRÉAS (VAUCLUSE) FRANCE
PRODUCE OF FRANCE

M. CHAPOUTIER

SAINT-JOSEPH

DESCHANTS

MARQUE DÉPOSÉE

APPELLATION St-JOSEPH CONTRÔLÉE

MIS EN BOUTEILLE PAR

M. CHAPOUTIER S.A.

NÉGOCIANTS-ÉLEVEURS A TAIN L'HERMITAGE DRÔME

e 75cl

RASTEAU

CÔTES DU RHÔNE VILLAGES

APPELLATION CÔTES DU RHÔNE VILLAGES CONTRÔLÉE

DOMAINE SAINT GAYAN

MIS EN BOUTEILLE AU DOMAINE

G.a.e.c. du Domaine Saint-Gayan à Gigondas (Vse) France

e 75cl

PRODUIT DE FRANCE

PRODUCT OF FRANCE

Côte-Rôtie

APPELLATION COTE-ROTIE CONTROLÉE

Côte Blonde ‹La Garde›

750ml

MISE EN BOUTEILLES A LA PROPRIÉTÉ

A. DERVIEUX-THAIZE, Propriétaire-Viticulteur, VERENAY-AMPUIS (Rhône) FRANCE

FAC ET SPERA

LA PETITE RUCHE

CROZES-HERMITAGE

APPELLATION CROZES-HERMITAGE CONTROLÉE

MIS EN BOUTEILLE PAR

M. Chapoutier S.A. e 75cl

NÉGOCIANTS-ÉLEVEURS, A TAIN-L'HERMITAGE (DROME)

FRANCE

A BUYER'S GUIDE

In addition to their 'appellation contrôlée' certain wines may use the name of a specific vineyard or domaine, or special cuvée on the label to distinguish their wines from the masses.

CELLIER DE L'ENCLAVE DES PAPES

PRODUCE OF FRANCE

CÔTES DU RHÔNE
APPELLATION CÔTES DU RHÔNE CONTRÔLÉE

TMI

MIS EN BOUTEILLE PAR
UNION DES VIGNERONS DE L'ENCLAVE DES PAPES A VALRÉAS VAUCLU.

PRODUCE OF FRANCE

Château de Beaucastel

CHATEAUNEUF-DU-PAPE
APPELLATION CHATEAUNEUF-DU-PAPE CONTROLÉE

Sté FERMIÈRE DES VIGNOBLES PIERRE PERRIN
AU CHATEAU DE BEAUCASTEL COURTHEZON (Vse)   75 cl
MIS EN BOUTEILLE DU CHATEAU

---

le Chevalier de Sterimberg
MARQUE   DEPOSÉE

HERMITAGE
APPELLATION HERMITAGE CONTRÔLÉE

PAUL JABOULET AÎNÉ
Mis en bouteilles par

75 cl

PAUL JABOULET AINÉ, NÉGOCIANT ÉLEVEUR A TAIN L'HERMITAGE DRÔME FRANCE

WHAT TO LOOK FOR

There is such a variety of wine from the Rhône valley that the first task when buying is to decide whether you want a high-class red for laying down to drink in the next decade, a few bottles to serve at an informal barbecue or a dessert wine to go with a special pudding. Identify the purpose and the purchase becomes much easier.

The next step is to decide which appellation to buy, and then which producers to choose. For everyday red wine, for example, Côtes du Rhône is a good choice, but it would be sad to ignore other deserving candidates such as Lirac, Coteaux du Tricastin or even the humble sounding (but usually very good) Vins de Pays de l'Ardèche. Price, availability, your past enjoyment of such names and other people's advice should guide your choice. Part of the fun of choosing wine is the challenge of the unknown or, put more mundanely, trial and error. This will allow you to build up your own detailed knowledge of different wine names.

While this book will help you to distinguish the regions of the Rhône valley and make familiar some of the better known producers' names, it is not possible to tell you exactly what to expect from each bottle. The label will not say, for instance, whether a Côtes du Rhône was made by *macération carbonique* or traditional fermentation methods, though there may be a back label giving some hints. A merchant's list, or the supermarket shelves, may offer more than one example of a particular appellation: how does one decide? The best idea is to take someone else's advice. You may be certain that a wine merchant who offers a wide selection of Rhône wines, with a number of different examples of each appellation, knows what he is talking about and will be able to help you with your choice. It will be in his interests to sell you a wine that suits your needs (rather than his) as you will then be more likely to return for a repeat purchase.

Choosing wine becomes simpler if you can taste before you buy. If you are prepared to purchase in cases, rather than single bottles, then it is no problem to persuade wine merchants to invite you to their tastings. Most of the wine warehouses, where you must purchase by the case, will offer wines to taste on their premises at any time during their opening hours. Joining a wine society is a relatively inexpensive way to try a wide variety of wines with like-minded people, with no commitment to buy.

Many derive enormous pleasure from buying their wine in the region of production. Here it will certainly be possible to taste. In the southern Rhône, every village has its own cooperative where you can taste before you buy. The cooperative at Tain in the north offers all the northern Rhône appellations so that you can choose. Alternatively, many merchants and growers advertise their wares on signs by the roadside, and will be delighted to discuss their latest vintages with you. Should you go to a grower's cellar, though, it is normally expected that you will buy unless you do not like their wine. Even so, it takes bravery and tact to criticize a producer's wines on his own territory, so be prepared to purchase.

Not all cellars will be open to such visits; they may not have much wine left to sell, nor have the resources to look after visitors. If a cellar does not advertise visits or tastings, ask and, if necessary, make an appointment for later. If the producer has wine to sell, he is unlikely to turn away a serious enquirer.

If you are going to taste more than a handful of wines, be prepared to spit out; your palate and judgement, not to mention your head, become jaded very quickly otherwise.

When tasting in the cellars, or even at home or in a restaurant, it is helpful to know what are genuine faults or problems. The first thing is the appearance of the wine. If white, it should be anything from very pale to deep yellow; if it is brown there is something wrong with it or it just may be too old. Red wines vary in colour from deep-purple to orangey-red; again a brown wine is faulty. The better the quality and higher the appellation, the deeper the colour. The colour lightens with age.

Pieces of cork in the wine do not mean a corked bottle; that rarity is easily recognizable by a most unpleasant, rotten, musty smell instead. Similarly, weeping or mouldy corks do not necessarily signify a fault; always wipe the neck of the bottle before pouring. A deposit in the bottle is no fault either; red wines usually throw a coloured deposit after some time in the bottle. Colourless crystals can occur in red or white wines exposed to cold weather after bottling.

Although unsightly in appearance, these crystals are perfectly natural and the wine can be decanted off them. Some producers prefer not to chill-stabilize their bulk wine in order to preserve the maximum amount of bouquet and flavour.

Any wine that smells seriously 'off' in any way – vinegary, musty, rotten or rancid – must be rejected; so should a wine that is cloudy (as opposed to having a few particles in it). A cloudy wine, or one that is fizzing, is likely to smell bad as well since it will be suffering from some microbiological or chemical contamination. A wine that smells good is likely to taste good, although excessive acidity, sweetness or tannin may not necessarily be detected on the nose.

In a restaurant it is acceptable to return a bottle if it is incorrectly served, at the wrong temperature for example. This is obviously not the fault of the wine; if it were served under the right conditions it might be most enjoyable.

With practice, it is relatively easy to decide if a wine is actually faulty, or whether it is simply that you did not like it. Red wines from the northern vineyards of the Rhône, tend to be very tannic when young. This usually bodes a long life ahead so, although the tannin may be unpleasant in the early stages, this does not necessarily reflect any fault or lack of quality in the wine. Similarly with high acidity in white wines; its preservative qualities stand the wine in good stead for the future, if it is a wine meant to be kept. Plenty of fruit and concentration are the important features to look for; these are necessary to balance the tannin and acidity.

UNDERSTANDING THE LABEL

Wine labels serve two purposes: first, to give information on the provenance of the wine and second, by means of an eyecatching design, to encourage people to buy. In days gone by, the second aim of the label often conflicted with the first; misleading information was put on to make the consumer think it was a better wine than it really was. Before EEC regulations governing wine labels were drawn up and enforced, any powerful red wine was in danger of being labelled Châteauneuf-du-Pape, regardless of its origin, as that was a name people recognized.

Happily the regulations have made such blatant fraud extremely unlikely. Each bottle of wine must carry certain items of information, and may mention certain others. The bottle must state the volume of the contents, normally 75 cl (the bottle size), 37.5 cl or 1.5 litre (half-bottle and magnum sizes respectively) or 1.0 litre. The label must also state the country of origin.

Other information which must appear on the label refers to the status of the wine. Wine labelled *Vin de Table* may not have any indication of which region it comes from. *Vin de Pays*, or a 'country wine' is *Vin de Table* but with a geographical origin: Vin de Pays du Gard, for example. *Vin Délimité de Qualité Supérieure*, or VDQS, wines represent a halfway house between table wine and full *appellation contrôlée* (AC) status; the wines are subject to certain rules in their production but these are less strict than for *appellation contrôlée*. Many VDQS areas eventually achieve promotion to full AC status, such as Côtes du Lube-

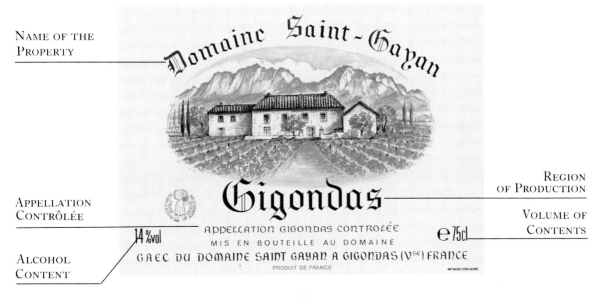

NAME OF THE PROPERTY

APPELLATION CONTRÔLÉE

ALCOHOL CONTENT

REGION OF PRODUCTION

VOLUME OF CONTENTS

NAME OF PROPERTY

VINTAGE

REGION OF PRODUCTION

PRIZES WON IN COMPETITION

ALCOHOL CONTENT

APPELLATION CONTRÔLÉE

VOLUME OF CONTENTS

WHERE THE WINE WAS BOTTLED

ron and Coteaux du Tricastin. VDQS wines will say *'Vin Délimité de Qualité Supérieure'* on the label, or even *'Appellation d'Origine Vin Délimité de Qualité Supérieure'* (not to be confused with *appellation contrôlée*), as well as the name of the region. *Appellation contrôlée* wines will give the region as well as the status, often with the name of the region repeated between the words *appellation* and *contrôlée*.

The AC areas of the Rhône valley must be specified on the label, though should a Côtes du Rhône-Villages wine come from just one village, the village name may appear on the label. For example, wines from Cairanne can be called 'Côtes du Rhône Cairanne, Appellation Côtes du Rhône-Villages Contrôlée'. Some appellations are village or town names – Condrieu, Gigondas, Tavel – while others describe a larger area: Côtes du Rhône, in particular. Some appellations refer to vineyards, such as Château Grillet, or viticulturally delimited districts, such as Hermitage or Côte Rôtie, rather than villages. *'Appellation contrôlée'* on the label does not guarantee quality, however, just authenticity.

It is now obligatory for all wine labels to state the alcoholic strength in percentage of alcohol by volume on the label, as this will help you to know whether to expect a light or heavy bodied wine. If a Châteauneuf-du-Pape, for example, is labelled as containing 14 degrees of alcohol, then you will know that it should be treated with respect.

The last piece of information that must go on a wine label is the name of the bottler, who may not necessarily be the producer if the wine is bottled by a

négociant or shipped in bulk and bottled by a British merchant. It is the bottler who is initially liable in case of fault, though any complaints should first be addressed to the merchant who supplied the wine. Domaine-bottled wines will often also carry the words *'mise en bouteille à la propriété'* or *'mise au domaine'*.

Certain other information may also appear on a wine label which will tell you something more about the wine. First, most wines can be expected to carry a vintage date which will not only tell you how old a wine is but also indicate the characteristics the wine may be expected to have (see *Vintages*, pages 33–34). A generic Côtes du Rhône or Châteauneuf-du-Pape may be blended to a consistent style every year, so the vintage date will tell you more about the state of maturity of the wine than its overall quality.

Names of individual domaines may be given on the label and the grape variety may be mentioned provided it comprises at least 85 per cent of the blend; in the Rhône valley this is only likely with Syrah, in the northern sector, though an interesting Chardonnay, Vin de Pays de l'Ardèche, has been made by a Burgundy *négociant* who has bought vineyards there.

Certain descriptive terms may also appear on the label, though these mainly relate to colour, and dryness or sweetness. Information regarding the style, details of the producer and how best to serve the wine may appear on a back label, and can be very helpful. Some back labels may also show a code, numbering from 1 (dry) to 9 (sweet) for white wines.

VINTAGES

Any attempt to generalize, or typecast, vintages usually ends in disaster as even in a poor vintage some good wines can be made; and in a good vintage bad producers will always make sub-standard wines. Vintage charts can never provide the whole story, but only give an indication of the general character of a certain year.

The Rhône valley seldom has a really bad vintage. This is not just because techniques in the vineyards have improved so that rot is no longer an inevitable corollary to rain, but also because the climate permits the grapes to ripen properly in virtually all years. The quality and style of a vintage mainly depend on the critical three or four last weeks of ripening before the harvest.

With the exception of Château Grillet and Hermitage blanc, most white Rhône wine ages quickly and is best drunk within two or three years of its production. Many red wines, particularly those based on the Grenache grape, are also made for early drinking. The Syrah grape may require extensive bottle ageing. The better northern Rhône reds are capable of outlasting many a good claret or red burgundy. Top-class Châteauneuf-du-Pape should also need three to four years or more in bottle.

1988 A mild winter followed by a damp spring led to a normal flowering in the south, although there was some rain in the north, reducing quantities by about 10 per cent (more in Côte Rôtie). A hot dry summer resulted in an early harvest with deep-coloured, full, alcoholic reds, which are concentrated and suitable for long keeping. White wines are full and aromatic. From the outset, quality in the north and south looks good, even great, comparable with the superb 1985.

1987 The vintage arrived late; white grapes were picked successfully and then there was rain, rain and more rain, particularly in the south. The critical final ripening of the red grapes was disturbed, giving very pale red wines. The sugar content of the grapes was reduced; 1987 was the first year since 1984 that chaptalization (enrichment of the must with sugar) was permitted. Wines from the northern Rhône vineyards were generally better than those of the south; the reds are judged better than 1986s with better colour and more fruit, flavour and richness.

1986 Both north and south experienced similar conditions: a cool spring nevertheless led to a normal flowering followed by an extremely hot summer.

In the north, red wines were abundant, fairly hard and tannic, occasionally lacking in richness but they will mature relatively early. In the south, the September rains resulted in grapes absorbing the water rapidly, sometimes even bursting. Grapes that were perfectly healthy one day could be split and rotten the next, so swift was the onset of the rot. Only those who were able to pick early made deep-coloured, alcoholic wines. In the higher vineyards, such as in the Côtes du Ventoux, there was no wind after the rain (usually the mistral is the saving grace in these circumstances) so the rot set in. Many growers needed to sort through their crop after picking.

In Châteauneuf, some excellent wines were made which will mature between 1992 and 2000.

1985 A hot summer with very little rainfall heralded a great vintage. The red wines of the north are ripe, tannic, deep-coloured and enormously concentrated. Cornas and Côte Rôtie are particularly good, with slightly less acidity and toughness than the highly regarded 1983s. Condrieu, too, made rich, powerful, ripe white wines.

In the south the crop was quite large. As early as mid-August, many grapes were overripe. During the harvest very hot temperatures gave difficulties in controlling fermentation for ill-equipped growers. Grapes in most areas were clean and healthy; with hindsight, top-class wines could have been made if yields had been limited and picking done earlier. Many good wines were made while others should have been better. There were plenty of big, alcoholic, low-acid wines that will not keep long.

1984 A great vintage such as 1983 is always a difficult act to follow. 1984 suffered from a bad press before the vintage, so that even the better wines struggled to attain recognition.

Many red wines in the north suffered from under-ripeness. The resultant high acidity in the white wines of Hermitage and Condrieu bodes well for their keeping qualities; on the whole the white wines are also delicate and subtle. The southern Rhône vineyards experienced plenty of rain before the harvest, giving austere though well-structured wines. In a year that was uniformly disappointing throughout France, Châteauneuf-du-Pape produced the best 1984 reds in the whole of the country.

1983 What a year! In the northern Rhône vineyards, a dry, hot summer produced modest quantities of rich, concentrated red wines with plenty of tannin, requiring at least another decade of cellaring to reveal their true potential. White wines in the north were also good; these are drinking well now.

In the south, the Grenache suffered from *coulure* during flowering, so the mixture of grapes in the blends is low in this variety. Those who did not destalk Syrah after picking found too much green astringence in the wines; normally the Grenache's vinosity counteracts this tendency. Châteauneuf-du-Pape experienced a variable vintage: the better made wines should keep. Gigondas made tannic, heavy, full-bodied wines of average to good quality.

1982 All France experienced excessive heat at vintage time, creating difficulties for producers without adequate cooling facilities.

In the north, the hot conditions gave full-bodied, low acid red wines which are almost ready to drink. Côte Rôtie produced some sensitive wines which are not for long ageing. White wines are ready now as the low acidity has allowed them to age rapidly.

The southern vineyards gave a large yield of fat, soft, almost overripe wines. Some Châteauneuf-du-Pape reds achieved alcoholic levels as high as 14.5 degrees. On the whole the wines are soft and fragile.

1981 Côte Rôtie and Hermitage did not receive the full warmth and sunshine hoped for, giving average quality wines. Cornas enjoyed slightly better weather and so less astringent wines were produced. Red wines are for drinking now until 1990. This is not a vintage with any real pedigree.

In the south, achieving sufficient ripeness was also a problem. Even so, Gigondas wines vary from average to excellent, depending on the producer, while Châteauneuf-du-Pape made rich, powerful wines with good balance and which were more consistent than the variable 1983s.

1980 Like 1984, 1980 was regarded as mediocre to start with, although many wines turned out much

better than previously imagined. In the northern Rhône, soft, approachable and well-balanced wines were made.

Châteauneuf-du-Pape produced some of the best wines in the whole of France in this year, as in 1984; with the emphasis on fruit and elegance rather than weight and fullness.

1979 Good whites were made in 1979 in Hermitage and Crozes-Hermitage. The reds were even better. Excellent colour, depth and balance characterize this vintage.

The southern Rhône 1979s are of excellent quality, in many cases matching that of the 1978s.

1978 For red wines, this vintage was undoubtedly the best since 1961. The top wines are still too closed and tannic and should be kept until the next decade to develop their enormous perfume and fruit. 1978 is generally judged to be even better than 1983. Who knows how long these wines will last?

For the southern wines, this was the best year since 1961 and 1967: a 'miracle' year, in that the sirocco wind set in just before the vintage, but the expected rains never came. 1978 challenges the opinion that southern Rhône wines age quickly; the Châteauneufs are just beginning to open up. They are showing fantastic balance, richness and opulence.

Older Vintages White wines should have all been drunk up by now, though the occasional Hermitage blanc may be enjoyed if cellared well.

Once over ten years old only exceptional southern reds and the better northern ones will still make enjoyable drinking. Vintages to look out for are 1976, 1972, 1971, 1970 and 1969. These last three are called *Les Trois Glorieuses* as three good years in a row were especially welcomed following a decade where four vintages (1960, 1963, 1965, 1968) were almost totally spoilt by excessive rain. 1967 was especially good in the south, though unexceptional in the north. Going back to older vintages, 1966, 1964 and 1961 were fine; the last of these was one of the great vintages this century, remembered alongside the legendary years of 1947 and 1929.

Earlier than 1961, only the wines from the better domaines will be in fine drinking form. Should you be so fortunate as to come across Jaboulet's Hermitage La Chapelle or Guigal's Côte Rôtie La Mouline, of almost any age, these are likely to have survived the course. Of the white wines, Chapoutier's Hermitage Blanc is notably long-lasting.

PRICE STRUCTURE

In any trade, prices are governed not only by quality but also by supply and demand: better known names normally command a higher price. A top estate Châteauneuf can command twice the price of a generic wine and be worth three or four times as much.

Wine prices are not only guided by availability but also by the weather. While the Rhône valley does have vintage variations, seldom is the quality so dreadful that it is difficult to sell. Prices are, therefore, much less sensitive than in some other wine-growing regions.

At the less expensive end of the price scale you can find plenty of satisfying wines at keen prices from the southern part of the Rhône valley. Lowest priced of all will be the *Vins de Pays*, of which the Rhône valley and its environs can offer an abundance.

Next will come the VDQS wines and some of the basic appellations of the south. The Côtes du Vivarais, Côtes du Luberon, Coteaux du Tricastin or Côtes du Ventoux, as well as the ubiquitous Côtes du Rhône, should provide reliable quality at an affordable price. However, not all wines bearing these names will be good – some can be awful. Stick to producers you can trust.

One satisfying aspect of the comparatively stable and favourable pricing of wines from the south, is that the premium asked for estate or domaine wines is often very small.

Moving up the price scale to the medium range, you can include some of the northern Rhône wines. Crozes-Hermitage can provide a good example of the Syrah for a comparatively small outlay.

The southern Rhône can offer many medium-priced wines. The unique Tavel rosé or a delicious herby red from its neighbour Lirac make satisfying drinking. Châteauneuf-du-Pape can command prices across a wide range. No one can expect to pay as much for a run-of-the-mill Châteauneuf as for a good vintage of Château de Beaucastel or Domaine du Vieux Télégraphe, nor indeed will the wines have much in common from the point of view of depth and concentration of aroma and flavour.

The very top wines are necessarily the rarest. Top-quality Côte Rôtie and Hermitage comes from vineyards that are difficult to work. Low yields and careful vinification followed by long ageing all cost money so these wines can never be cheap. But what magnificent value they represent in comparison with top Bordeaux or burgundies! The very best wines can now be purchased in advance in the spring following the vintage, *en primeur*. This method of buying allows the purchaser to obtain excellent wines at the opening price. The wines are likely to appreciate in value so this is a good way to invest in the greatest vintages. Hermitage and Côte Rôtie are produced in quantities twenty or thirty times less than those of Châteauneuf-du-Pape; necessarily they will be more expensive, though not always better.

Condrieu and Château Grillet are only available in minute quantities as small areas are planted and serious hazards are involved in obtaining a successful crop of the Viognier grape. Their asking prices reflect their rarity.

Different occasions warrant a variety of wine styles, and indeed expenditure. The Rhône valley can cater for them all.

PRICE GUIDE

INEXPENSIVE
Vin de Pays
Côtes du Rhône
Côtes du Rhône-Villages
Côtes du Ventoux
Coteaux du Tricastin
Côtes du Vivarais

MIDDLE RANGE
Tavel
Lirac
Gigondas
Châteauneuf-du-Pape (generic wines)
Crozes-Hermitage
St-Joseph
Cornas
Muscat de Beaumes-de-Venise
St-Péray

TOP-CLASS
Côte Rôtie
Hermitage
Condrieu
Château Grillet
Châteauneuf-du-Pape (better domaines)

THROUGH
THE
VINEYARDS

*The massive bulk of the Mont Ventoux dominates
the plain below where the unrelenting mistral wind
has made the vines grow on a slant.*

NORTHERN RHÔNE

As the Rhône valley is divided into two discrete sections, two separate tours of the vineyards may be made. Here we begin with the northern Rhône vineyards.

CÔTE RÔTIE

Côte Rôtie produces one of the world's finest red wines, though few realize it; wines of enormous power and perfume, yet voluptuous and elegant.

Côte Rôtie means literally the 'roasted slope' or, less romantically, the 'burnt hillside'. Its name not only reflects the dark colour and warm, robust flavour of the wine, but serves as a reminder that it represents the beginning of the vineyards that bask in the hot, dry climate which only starts south of Lyon. After twenty miles or so of driving down the autoroute from Lyon, suddenly the congested industrial surroundings give way to strikingly steep hills and green countryside at Ampuis. The South of France starts here.

Local opinion differs regarding the origin of the vines at Côte Rôtie; what is certain is that the Romans were the first to make wine of any consequence. Here the wine drunk locally was known as *vinum picatum*, which can be translated as a wine with a taste of pitch, and was reputed to be coarse, powerful in body and deep in colour. Although not a particularly attractive description, it illustrates quite neatly the basic character of the wine, nowadays vastly improved.

The vineyards themselves are among the steepest in France, their 55° slopes comparing with those of Germany's Mosel and Portugal's Douro valley regions. The rock base is granitic, with varying topsoils according to the location of the vineyards. Under such conditions erosion of the topsoil and the sheer physical difficulty of working on such precipitous slopes necessitated the building of stonewalled terraces. These were constructed by the Romans and still remain today. Even abandoned and overgrown vineyards often still exhibit the terracing structure.

These steep slopes must necessarily be worked by hand as the narrow terraces preclude the use of any machines. Mules and horses are sometimes used in the vineyards, though most work is done manually, with the help of pulleys. Obviously the high cost in terms of time and skilled labour puts Côte Rôtie at a commercial disadvantage, with the result that some vineyards are no longer planted. Any vineyard expansion to satisfy the increasing world demand for Côte Rôtie has been on the plateau behind. Although this is still officially within the *appellation contrôlée* delimited area, these vineyards are less well placed than those on the hillsides, whose favourable aspect and gravity-assisted drainage confer an obvious advantage.

The vines are tended in a different manner from those in neighbouring appellations, because of the steepness, using a modification of the *guyot* method, called the *taille Côte Rôtie*. The vine is supported on four stakes of differing lengths, and the shoots that will bear the fruit are led outwards along these sticks to obtain the best exposure to the sun. Syrah comprises the majority, about 90 per cent of the plantation. Although Côte Rôtie may include up to 20 per cent of the white grape, Viognier, many growers no longer use it as it is so difficult to grow. No white wine is made in Côte Rôtie.

The Côte Rôtie vineyards are planted on two hillsides above Ampuis, known as the Côte Brune and the Côte Blonde. The names stem from the legend of the feudal lord, Maugiron, who lived in the château of Ampuis and is said to have bequeathed the two slopes to his beautiful daughters, one with golden blonde hair, the other a ravishing brunette. The wines from each hill are certainly different: the Côte Blonde has a limestone-based soil and produces lighter, more lively, less tannic wines than the Côte Brune where the soil has more clay, iron and sand. Côte Brune wines are more reticent when young, develop slowly but have greater staying power. Virtually all the Viognier planted is on the Côte Blonde, for it does not flourish in the heavier, clay soil of the Côte Brune. Very little Côte Rôtie is actually bottled and sold from just one Côte; the vast majority is a blend of the two. A few vineyards, such as Guigal's La Mouline on the Côte Blonde and Dervieux-Thaize's La Viaillère from the Côte Brune, make wine of sufficiently good quality to be sold individually. Such wines will only be available in very small quantities; the total area under vines in Côte Rôtie is just 130 hectares/320 acres, the size of a

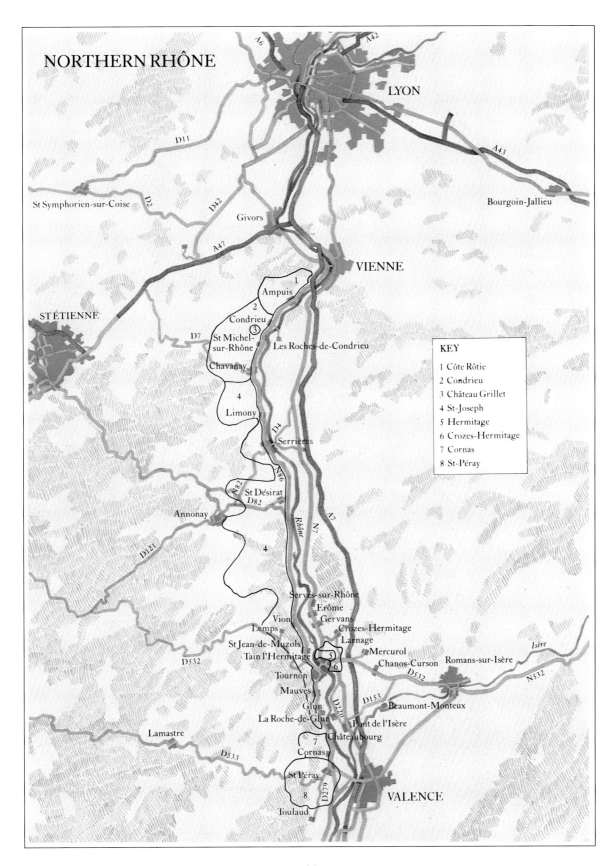

NORTHERN RHÔNE

LYON

St Symphorien-sur-Coise

Givors

VIENNE

Bourgoin-Jallieu

ST ÉTIENNE

Ampuis

1

2
Condrieu
3
St Michel-
sur-Rhône

Les Roches-de-Condrieu

Chavanay

4

Limony

Serrières

St Désirat

Annonay

4

KEY

1 Côte Rôtie
2 Condrieu
3 Château Grillet
4 St-Joseph
5 Hermitage
6 Crozes-Hermitage
7 Cornas
8 St-Péray

Serves-sur-Rhône
Erôme
Gervans

Vion
Lemps

Crozes-Hermitage
Larnage

St Jean-de-Muzols
Tain l'Hermitage

Mercurol
Chanos-Curson

Romans-sur-Isère

5
6

Isère

Tournon

Mauves

Glun

La Roche-de-Glun

Beaumont-Monteux

Pont de l'Isère

Lamastre

Châteaubourg

7
Cornas

St Péray

8

VALENCE

Toulaud

single domaine in the southern Côtes du Rhône.

The Côte Rôtie vintage usually takes place near the end of September. The grapes are hand-picked and placed in bulky wooden holders, the *beneaux*, which are passed from person to person down to the bottom of the hillside. From there they are taken to the press houses.

Traditionally, large oak vats have been used for fermentation, but they are relatively difficult to clean properly and temperature control is not easy. As a result, a trend towards lined metal or stainless steel is beginning, led by Marcel Guigal. Guigal has also pioneered the use of new oak barrels for maturing the wine. New oak, widely used in the best burgundies and Bordeaux, can allow a potentially complex wine to develop its secondary aromas, but the powerful vanilla character of new oak can also mask the short-comings of an indifferent wine. As Guigal's wines are among the finest of the appellation, this criticism cannot be levelled at him.

A young Côte Rôtie when bottled will be deep purple in colour, which changes to ruby red only slowly. A good Côte Rôtie can take years to mature: eight years plus for an average vintage, and up to twenty for the very best years. It has a harsh, acrid, smoky, peppery aroma when young, though as the wine matures, the smoother, blackberry fruit and violet perfumes begin to assert themselves and the elegance and finesse of the wine can be assessed. Côte Rôtie is naturally a tannic wine, though the levels of tannin vary considerably from year to year. The addition of the white Viognier grape produces a somewhat softer, more flowery, elegant wine than those of Hermitage on the other side of the river; however, today the trend is more and more towards making wines with 100 per cent Syrah although Marcel Guigal does add a little of the press wine from his Condrieu to his Côte Rôtie.

Guigal makes four different Côte Rôties: a regular *cuvée* which is a Brune–Blonde blend, the famous Côte Blonde La Mouline and the (less well-known) Côte Brune counterpart, La Landonne. That name is also shared by René Rostaing, another top grower. The fourth Guigal wine, La Turque, comes from a tiny plot on the Côte Brune. It has only been made since 1985, the first release being in 1988. The three vineyard-designated *cuvées* spend a record forty-two months in the new barrels, with no fining or filtra-tion, only racking. All of the wines are fermented with the stalks in to give extra backbone to them. All the Guigal Côte Rôties are characterized by huge in-tensity, from the velvety but powerful La Mouline to

the solid, tannic, peppery, more masculine La Lan-donne, all with massive fruit.

Few of the other good producers believe in new wood to the extent that Guigal does. Robert Jasmin has no wood younger than two to three years old to mature his wines. Unlike Guigal, he has eliminated all Viognier from his wine. Whereas Guigal's wines have enormous depth of aroma and flavour, Jasmin's Côte Rôtie is more elegant and supple, easy to drink even when young, and splendidly ripe.

Neither Marius Gentaz-Dervieux nor his brother-in-law Albert Dervieux-Thaize use new barrels, though an experimental one has been spotted in the latter's cellars. Dervieux-Thaize makes very traditional Côte Rôtie: La Viaillère from the old vines on the Côte Brune, La Garde from medium-aged vines on the Côte Blonde, and Fongent from 15-year-old (or less) vines from the Côte Brune. He too leaves the stalks in and his wines are never filtered though they are fined with egg-whites. They are very tannic and unapproachable in their youth, but mature into strong, masculine, rich wines that last particularly well. His wines are more solid than those of Jasmin, for example. The solidity of this wine was demonstrated to great effect recently. Albert Dervieux sent a consignment of his wine to San Francisco. For some reason it was delayed and spent the best part of three months waiting on the dockside in searing heat, as did some burgundy going to the same importer. A rough sea voyage fol-lowed; M. Dervieux's wine was pronounced to be exactly as tasted in the cellars near Ampuis on arrival in California. The burgundy, however, was not so fortunate and was completely spoilt.

Gentaz-Dervieux's wines are also traditionally made and see twenty to twenty-two months in old oak before bottling. His wines are more elegant and less tannic than those of either his brother-in-law or Gui-gal, but are deeper coloured and more intense than those of Jasmin.

CÔTE RÔTIE	
Top Producers	**Other Recommended Producers**
Gentaz-Dervieux	M. Chapoutier
E. Guigal (incorporating	Delas Frères
Vidal-Fleury)	Paul Jaboulet Aîné
Robert Jasmin	Gilles & Pierre Barge
René Rostaing	Bernard Burgaud
Albert Dervieux-Thaize	Emile Champet
	Joseph Jamet

*Syrah, in Côte Rôtie, only survives on these
steep slopes if supported by stakes.*

CONDRIEU

Condrieu has to be included amongst France's, or indeed the world's, most esoteric white wines. To start with, the grape that produces Condrieu, the Viognier, is little grown anywhere outside the Rhône valley. Where it first came from is an intriguing matter. Some say the Phocaean Greeks brought it from Marseille, though it looks more likely to have been brought from Dalmatia in Yugoslavia by the Roman Emperor Probus in AD 281. Whatever the true origin of the Viognier, it is known that the Romans in Vienne drank wine from Condrieu at this time; their description of 'the violet perfume of the wines of Vienne', however, is ambiguous; it could have applied equally to red or white wine. As it is, no red wine is now made in Condrieu.

Condrieu is located south of Côte Rôtie's vineyards on the western bank of the Rhône river. The village of Condrieu was once known as Coin du Ruisseau, or corner of the stream, as it is situated on a bend in the river at the bottom of the terrace slopes, among fruit trees and lush green undergrowth; its situation is quiet and peaceful. Across the river, the sister village of Les Roches de Condrieu offers one of the very few safe beaches beside the turbulent water.

The Condrieu appellation extends over four communes altogether: Condrieu itself and, to the south, Vérin, St Michel-sur-Rhône and Limony, not counting Château Grillet, further south, a separate appellation. These are all very small villages, interconnected by tiny twisting lanes. Although the slopes of the Condrieu vineyards are almost as steep as those of Côte Rôtie and are similarly rock-based, the topsoil is totally different. So it is that the Viognier grape fares better here. The very fine topsoil consists of decomposed mica, known locally as *arzelles*, which is easily eroded and washed to the bottom of the hill in heavy rains, after which it needs to be carried up again. That and the steepness of the slopes has moderated further planting in the area.

Only about 12 hectares/30 acres of vineyards are planted. The maximum permitted yield is 30 hectolitres per hectare, though the average production is only 20. Added to such a small production is the difficulty of getting the Viognier to grow successfully. The combination of these factors means that Condrieu can never be a cheap wine, and because production is so small demand inevitably exceeds supply. The wine has to be sold on allocation as most top-class restaurants in France wish to list it.

The white wines of Condrieu are exotic and complex. The Viognier grape gives a full-bodied, pale-gold wine with a delicate aroma of peaches, pears, honeysuckle and apricots when mature, elusive and difficult to describe, but with a spicy earthiness when young. Normally it is vinified dry. It is a wine that is low in acidity and therefore matures quickly; it is usually bottled six months after the vintage. Local opinion differs on the subject of Condrieu's keeping qualities, though most advocate drinking the wine young while it is still lively and vivacious. Aged Condrieu can be a remarkable experience if the wine was of good quality to start with; a wine that is just six to seven years old can be expected to be deep golden in colour, with a bouquet that opens out to give a quite remarkable cornucopia of fruit aromas, particularly of apricot skins. Older Condrieu is for sipping and tasting; it is far too complex to drink freely. Only the very best wines age this well, and normally it is recommended that Condrieu be drunk well before it is five years old.

The tiny villages in the commune of Condrieu are worth
exploring for their views and scenery. Vines cover the south-facing slopes.
In Vérin you find many beautiful houses.

With such a small area under vines, there are only a few producers in the region. Georges Vernay owns by far the biggest share, having 6 hectares/15 acres which produce half the region's output of wine. M. Vernay ferments all his wine in stainless steel tanks and allows it to undergo the malolactic fermentation. A very small proportion of his wine comes from the excellent Coteaux de Vernon, though his regular bottling is still of superb quality. He uses new oak barrels for maturation, but with care; the delicate finesse of the wine could otherwise easily be masked by the powerful character of new oak. Jean Pinchon, by contrast, uses well-seasoned oak barrels that have seen many vintages, giving his wine nearly two years ageing in wood. Marcel Guigal makes his Condrieu with a mixture of ancient and modern: 40 per cent of his wine receives three months in new oak while the rest remains in stainless steel tanks. The wines are then blended together and bottled in April following the vintage. As only some of his wine has been in oak

barrels, the toasty, vanilla flavours are not overwhelming.

A relative newcomer to the Condrieu growers is Paul Multier, who owns the Château du Rozay estate comprising just 1 hectare/2.4 acres of vineyard on the Coteau de Chèry, a well-appointed site on the Condrieu hillside behind the town itself. Here the grapes are usually harvested late, to obtain a degree of overripeness. As a result, his wine is intense, rich and exotic but requires drinking within fours years as there is insufficient acidity for long ageing.

CONDRIEU	
Top Producers	**Other Recommended Producers**
Delas Frères	Paul Multier
Etienne Guigal	Jean Pinchon
Georges Vernay	André Dézormeaux
	Pierre Barge

Although Condrieu is essentially a dry wine, it has in the past been made sweet and sparkling, though this version has gone out of fashion. The sweet wine has its fermentation arrested prematurely with sulphur to kill off the wine yeasts. The dry wine is generally considered to be far superior, as the sugar in the sweet variety overwhelms its delicate perfume. Georges Vernay makes one called Vin de Noël for his family and certain private customers and André Dézormeaux makes a little for friends and neighbours; otherwise sweet Condrieu is seldom found.

CHÂTEAU GRILLET

Château Grillet is well known as France's smallest appellation. In terms of grape variety and vineyard location, the wine resembles Condrieu but is otherwise very different. As with Condrieu, only white wine is produced.

This tiny vineyard is situated 160 metres/175 yards above the river valley but below the village of St Michel-sur-Rhône, a mile or so south of Condrieu; it used to be only 2.28 hectares (less than 6 acres) in size but was expanded to almost 3 hectares in 1971. Only 1000 cases of wine are made each year, at the very most. It enjoys a favourable situation; the rows of Viognier vines are planted in the form of an amphitheatre facing south-south-east, where they benefit from the full warmth of the sun while enjoying protection from the wind by the steep hillside surrounding it.

The soil, similar to that of Condrieu, is lighter and more friable, again containing tiny fragments of decomposed mica (though there is more here than in Condrieu).

Château Grillet has always been in the possession of the Neyrat-Gachet family. Since 1830 they have owned the property, extended over the years by successive owners and which includes a Louis XIII château.

The grapes are picked by hand in only three days and carefully brought to the cellars from the steep vineyard ledges that are so difficult to negotiate. Generally the harvest takes place early in October, in order not to risk the weather breaking to bring the autumn rains. It is debatable whether the early harvest allows the wine to develop its full potential in terms of richness and flavour, but its acidity will be higher and so it should have greater staying power.

The beautiful façade of the château conceals modern cellars below with a pneumatic press and stainless steel vats. The juice is fermented after pressing the grapes and the wine left on its lees till midwinter to develop extra subtle flavours. It is then racked into oak barrels, where it will remain for eighteen months before bottling. During this time the warm spring will bring about the malolactic fermentation and the subsequent cold winter will clarify the wine. The wine is kept for a few months after bottling before being released for sale.

The wine of Château Grillet is more delicate than most Condrieu wines, although it can attain 15 degrees alcohol by virtue of the sun-trapping bowl-shape of the vineyard. Its bouquet has been said to resemble apricots, spring flowers, truffles and honey; the elusive Viognier aromas defy accurate description. Unlike Condrieu, Château Grillet has the potential for ageing. M. Neyrat-Gachet recommends it to be drunk between the ages of five and eight years.

In the last ten years there has been a decline in the quality of the wine as it has apparently become lighter, greener and less rich. This could be due to several reasons. The planting of new vines in 1971 would mean that a percentage of the crop is coming from comparatively young vines which will not provide the richness and intensity of flavour that old ones can; this situation can only improve with time. Second, the relatively early harvest results in lighter, less ripe wines than a later picking. Third, such is the demand for Château Grillet that there must be a temptation to obtain the highest yields possible; recent years have seen a doubling of production though the new plantings do not account for a similar increase in the area under vines. Furthermore, these plantings are outside the classic amphitheatre, so trap the sun less well. The appellation only permits 32 hectolitres per hectare, which will virtually be reached if the full 1000 cases is made. Keeping the yield rather lower may ensure better quality, though with such a capricious grape as the Viognier, the desire to make the most of what will grow is fully understandable.

The wine is bottled in a distinctive dark yellow-brown bottle; up to now this has only been in the 70 centilitre size, rather incongruous for one of France's top wines. This changed in early 1989, as all wines produced and sold within the EEC must, by law, be in the larger 75 centilitre size. The bottle emphasizes the rarity value of Château Grillet, which sells at prices at least two to three times higher than that of the very finest Condrieus, a level that is difficult to justify. Therefore, for those of moderate means, Château Grillet must remain a curiosity to try just once in a lifetime.

Château Grillet's vineyard has superb exposure to the sun,
with a splendid view over the Rhône valley below. The terracing
of the vines is a common sight throughout the northern Rhône.

HERMITAGE

The Hermitage appellation begins at Tain l'Hermitage, about 48 kilometres/30 miles south of Condrieu on the opposite side of the river. Directly to the east of Tain is the splendid hill of Hermitage, which rises majestically above a curve in the river. It dominates the view from Tournon, Tain's sister town.

In the northern Rhône appellations, only Hermitage and the adjoining Crozes-Hermitage vineyards are situated on the eastern side of the river and only these sites have the same granite-based rock that is found on the other side in Côte Rôtie, St-Joseph and Cornas.

Hermitage vies with Côte Rôtie as the most expensive red wine from the northern Rhône and its white wines also fetch a good price. This is not just due to the quality – there is not much of it either. Only 125 hectares/310 acres are planted with vines, three-quarters of which go to make red wine; no more than the production of a single estate in Châteauneuf-du-Pape.

At the top of the hill is the tiny chapel of St Christopher, built by the holy knight Gaspard de Stérimberg. The chapel has been reconstructed and is now the property of the Jaboulet family, who call their best red and white Hermitage wines La Chapelle and

Chevalier de Stérimberg respectively, although the building is actually surrounded by Chapoutier-owned vines!

Hermitage's wines have had mixed fortunes. Early in the nineteenth century its red wines were the most expensive in France, and much sought after. At the end of this century the ravages of phylloxera brought this period of prosperity to an end and Hermitage has never reached the heights of popularity since. Though its reputation has lately been increasing, the price of the wines is well below that of the better clarets and burgundies, although Hermitage can outlive virtually all of them.

The granitic rock of Hermitage is covered with a topsoil of decomposed flint and chalk. The red Syrah grape is the most widely planted, though in parts there are more clayey patches which are suitable for planting the white grapes, Marsanne and Roussanne. The delicate Viognier is not planted here.

The hill is well situated in respect of the weather. South-west-facing, the slopes obtain maximum exposure benefiting from the last rays of the setting sun long after the vineyards on the west bank are in shadow. The granite soil also retains the heat of the sun, with the result that the average mean temperature in the vineyards is 13°C/56°F, warmer than would be expected in this area.

The hill itself consists of several different slopes divided into specific vineyard sites, with variations in the soil across the whole area. The northernmost slope is Les Bessards, on crystalline granite rock, which gives the deepest coloured, most concentrated tannic wines. Le Méal, adjoining Les Bessards to the south-east, contains some alluvial deposits as well as granitic soil; these wines are considered even better: they are full-bodied, fragrant and supple rather than powerful and tannic. Les Greffieux, at the bottom of the hill below Le Méal and directly behind Tain, has some schist as well as granite; its wines are, therefore, lighter, more velvety and scented than Les Bessards' wines. White grapes are also planted in the vineyard of Les Greffieux.

The other famous white wine vineyards include Les Rocoules, Les Murets, Les Donnières and Chante-Alouette. Chante-Alouette is owned exclusively by Chapoutier; it is situated higher up the slope than either Les Rocoules or Les Murets, and is just west of Le Méal. At Les Murets chalk and some flint favours white wine production. Lower down, Les Donnières produces wines of elegance and finesse, while Les Rocoules gives more classic, nutty, solid whites. The famous vineyard of La Chapelle is right at the top of the hill, although Paul Jaboulet Aîné do not own all of that site.

Like their counterparts in Côte Rôtie, most Hermitage producers do not give a vineyard designation to their wines, but prefer to make a blend from numerous small parcels of land from all over the area. Some wines do, however, specify a name. As well as Chapoutier's white Chante-Alouette, there is Sorrel's white Hermitage Les Rocoules and his Le Gréal, a red wine that is a blend from Le Méal and Les Greffieux. Most producers of red Hermitage feel that, for their regular bottling, a blend from different sites is the best practice, and this way they can also produce greater volumes. Several choose to sell their wine under a brand name, such as Chapoutier's Hermitage La Sizeranne (red), Delas' Cuvée Marquise de la Tourette (red and white) and Ferraton's Cuvée Le Reverdy (white) and Cuvée Les Miaux (red). These *cuvées* should not be mistaken for single vineyard wines, though they may well be of better quality than all but the very best of the latter.

Red Hermitage is generally made in traditional fashion, with wooden vats and old oak barrels being the order of the day. Delas Frères in Tournon have more modern equipment than many; all the ageing cellars are air-conditioned, even those containing small oak barrels and large wooden *foudres*. As in Côte Rôtie new oak does not get much of a look-in for Hermitage though Gérard Chave and Jean-Louis Grippat have confessed to buying one and three new barrels respectively, in both cases for experimental purposes. The feeling is generally that Hermitage contains all the concentration in the right balance to have natural longevity and development without the assistance of new oak.

A long fermentation for red wines, with the must in contact with the grape skins, is followed by a maturation period in wood, from several months to three and a half years (as practised by Guigal). The appellation laws allow 15 per cent of white wine to be included in red Hermitage, though few producers use any at all, and those that do use less than 5 per cent. Most believe that the best wines are made from 100 per cent Syrah.

A good Hermitage will be virtually unapproachable before it is five years old; it will then be a deep, dark, purply red colour with a bitter chocolate, peppery, closed-up, raw blackberry bouquet. The wine is difficult to taste young. The Syrah grape needs time to display its fruit and finesse once the tannin has begun to subside, and this is never more true than in the wines of Hermitage, which can live to forty years or more in the finest vintages. Then the wine has a rounded, complex smoky bouquet and a rich, velvety, supple flavour that lingers long in the mouth.

About 25 per cent of Hermitage wine is white, made from the Marsanne and Roussanne grape varieties. Since Roussanne is more difficult to grow, Marsanne is the dominating variety, although new disease-resistant clones of Roussanne are beginning to appear. White Hermitage is made in traditional fashion by and large (except for Paul Jaboulet); it too sees some time in small oak barrels before bottling. Good Hermitage should be pale when young, with a perfume of peaches or apricots, and nuttiness, with a slight smokiness that develops and mellows with age. The wines are always dry, but with great depth and fullness, and have sufficient acidity and richness to permit a long life; an eight-year-old wine can still be very much in its prime and certain wines may live even longer. A 1955 Hermitage blanc from Chapoutier tasted in 1983 was deep orangey gold in colour, yet still retained plenty of fruit, richness and interest. Their 1929 white is still magnificent, whereas the red of the same year faded long ago.

Curiously, Jaboulet's white, Le Chevalier de Stérimberg, is much lighter; he uses modern, cool-fermentation methods and no wood. His wines are squeaky clean but do not show much complexity or staying power.

Hermitage is also the source of a curious sweet wine called Vin de Paille, made in tiny quantities. Its name, translated as straw wine, derives from the practice of leaving late-picked grapes out on straw mats to dry into raisins with a huge sugar content before being pressed and vinified. The resultant wine will be sweet and rich, with an alcoholic strength of around 17 degrees. Vin de Paille dates back at least to before the nineteenth century, probably much earlier; the little that is still made in the region today comes mainly from the cellars of Chave, Chapoutier and Ferraton.

The best quality red Hermitages are dominated by both *négociants* and growers. Of the good *négociants*, Paul Jaboulet Aîné and Chapoutier are both based in Tain, while Delas Frères have premises across the river in Tournon, and the firm of Etienne Guigal is based in Ampuis in the Côte Rôtie. All of these *négociants*, except Guigal, own vineyards in Hermitage, but also buy grapes from other growers.

Without question, Paul Jaboulet's Hermitage La Chapelle is one of the world's greatest red wines. It is an extremely powerful wine that needs fifteen years or more to mature, and lives almost for ever. New

The hill of Hermitage rises steeply above the town of Tain and the river.
Several vineyard owners in this region take advantage of the terraces to display
their names on the hill, which is better for publicity than it is for the view!

Hermitage's hill varies in steepness, contours and aspect across its height and breadth, accounting for the different styles of wine that can be obtained from just one grape variety.

oak is not used but the wine spends just over a year in one- or two-year-old barrels, so some muted oakiness is apparent. The wine is deep-coloured, ripe and tannic – in other words it has masses of everything. Chapoutier and Guigal, by contrast, give their wines at least two-and-a-half years in old wood, but both make softer, less tannic wines. Chapoutier's is sometimes lean and light, but has ripe, spicy fullness in good years, whereas Guigal's is one of the deepest coloured Hermitages available. Delas have surprisingly modern cellars, giving very clean wines with lots of flesh and ripeness. The high proportion of wine from Les Bessards results in good depth and concentration.

Gérard Chave is undoubtedly the best of the growers. His wine spends nearly two years in barrel, and is almost as long-lasting as La Chapelle, although it matures after just seven to eight years. This wine is delicious in average years and superb in great vintages with excellent balance of acidity, fruit and ripeness. Chave's wine has more finesse but less intensity than Paul Jaboulet's; theirs are two of the best red wines France can offer.

Marc Sorrel, since taking his estate over from his father in 1982, now makes delightfully stylish, aromatic wines. Their soft, velvety exterior conceals a solid backbone of tannin that ages well. Michel Ferraton, another of the top growers, makes a wine with less tannin; a rich, soft, supple wine with masses of fruit and gamey flavours.

The *Cave Coopérative des Vins Fins* at Tain is by far the largest and most important of the three *caves coopératives* in the northern Rhône. Between them 540 members produce a quarter of the wine under the Hermitage appellation, as well as wines from the other appellations in the north such as Cornas. Unusually for a cooperative, it owns small oak barrels to age the wines and employs a cooper full time to make and repair them.

HERMITAGE	
Top Producers	**Other Recommended Producers**
Paul Jaboulet Aîné Jean-Louis Chave* M. Sorrel*	Cave Coopérative at Tain E. Guigal M. Chapoutier* Delas Frères* Jean-Louis Grippat* B. Faurie Jean & Michel Ferraton
* = good white wines	

CROZES-HERMITAGE

In the eyes of the layman the reputation of Crozes-Hermitage has long benefited from its proximity to Hermitage itself. Like Hermitage, Crozes-Hermitage produces both red and white wine, though not quite in the same class. In 1846 the tasting panel at the Lyon Wine Congress observed that, 'If they are not brothers, then they are certainly first cousins.' A fair judgement, as Crozes-Hermitage wines, reds in particular, lack some of the finesse, concentration and balance that Hermitage can offer, besides having considerably shorter lives.

The *appellation contrôlée* area covers eleven villages. Tain l'Hermitage forms the centre; to the north are Gervans, Larnage, Erôme, Servès and Crozes-Hermitage itself, to the east Mercurol and Chanos-Curson, and to the south Beaumont-Monteux, Pont-de-l'Isère and La Roche de Glun. The appellation covers 4800 hectares/12000 acres, but only about 800 hectares/1970 acres are planted, though this is an increase of some 50 per cent in the last fifteen years. The appellation produces six times as much wine as Hermitage.

The vineyards all surround the hill of Hermitage, so experience similar climatic conditions, though they do not rise so far in height, nor are they on the steepest slopes. The same grapes are planted: Syrah for red wines, Marsanne and Roussanne (mainly the former) for whites. The difference between the wines of Crozes-Hermitage and Hermitage is mainly attributable to the soil. The hard, granite rock of Hermitage gives way lower down the hill to sandier, more clayey, heavier soils, though the exact nature of the soil varies across the appellation. The better red wines come from Larnage and Gervans in the north, where the vineyards are on well-exposed hillsides overlooking the river valley. The topsoil is granitic at Gervans, which has a very similar situation to Hermitage, but is heavier and contains more clay at Larnage. White wines are best from the vineyards on the slopes near Mercurol, where the lighter, sandier soil better suits the Marsanne and Roussanne vines, though it can result in some very elegant red wines.

Elsewhere in the appellation the vineyards are flatter and more easily cultivated, making it possible to use machinery – the only place in the northern Rhône where this is so. For this reason most of the vineyard expansion is taking place in the flat regions towards Pont-de-l'Isère.

Red Crozes-Hermitage is traditionally vinified in the same manner as red Hermitage, using 100 per cent Syrah, though the must is not kept in contact with the skins for so long. It has always been remarkably forward in comparison to Hermitage and recently two-year-old wines have not only been widely available on wine-merchants' shelves but drinkable to boot, although a little further bottle age would be desirable. The forwardness of these wines can partly be explained by experimentation with the *macération carbonique* method of vinification, previously the preserve of the south. In particular the *cave coopérative* at Tain l'Hermitage tried this method to produce early drinking wines. In the past few years they have been making better-structured wines than when their experiments first began.

It is possible that more concentrated red wines could be made by restricting the yields of the Crozes vines, currently 50 hectolitres per hectare compared with 40 for Hermitage, and vinifying traditionally with a long *cuvaison*, the wine's confinement in the vat with the skins. The comparatively low prices obtainable for Crozes in comparison with Hermitage, 13 francs per bottle as opposed to over 50 francs at the time of writing, do, however, remove much of the incentive to make very fine wine. Those that do include Paul Jaboulet Aîné, whose Domaine de Thalabert in the commune of Crozes is a fine example of the potential of the Syrah grape. No white wine is made on this estate. This wine spends nearly a year in oak barrels before bottling, and is unusual among red Crozes-Hermitage in that it is judged to need between four and eight years to reach its peak. Jaboulet also makes a regular *cuvée* from wine purchased all over the appellation. Other 'old-style' red producers include Pierre Ferraton and Jules Fayolle, whose vineyards near Gervans produce good quality wine that is traditionally made. Of the wines that fall in the opposite category of soft, approachable, fruity and early-drinking, good ones are made at the Cave des Clairmonts, whose spicy, fresh wines represent excellent value. Softer wines also can be found at the *cave coopérative* at Tain, where the wines have shown better structure recently, and the Collange family's Domaine la Négociale. M. Tardy and Mme. Ange, previously from the cooperative at Tain, set up a domaine called Gaec de la Syrah nearly ten years ago making both red and white wines in a commercial style. Their red wine receives up to eighteen months' wood ageing, though the wines are fresh and supple.

White wine accounts for approximately a tenth of the Crozes-Hermitage appellation. Generally these are best when young, as their fresh fruitiness is preferable to the tired, heavy style of older wines. White

The local authorities like to inform visitors exactly which villages in the area produce wine.

wines are made in similar fashion to white Hermitage: a short sojourn in wood forms part of the recipe, though this can depress the natural liveliness of the wine and only works with the better quality ones. Modern methods, where fermentation temperatures are carefully controlled and wines bottled shortly after the vintage, are now being practised, largely successfully. Of the traditional style white wines, good examples may be found from Chapoutier, who makes fat, fleshy wines that still retain plenty of fruit, Jules Fayolle (though quantities are limited to 100 cases), Paul Jaboulet Aîné from their own vineyards (the wine is called La Mule Blanche) and Delas Frères, whose white Crozes wines are surprisingly powerful and aromatic. The Cave des Clairmonts produces a very commercial white wine of the modern style, as do the Collanges, whose estate is favourably situated on the sandy soil of Mercurol. Tardy & Ange make a cool fermented fresh white wine from 100 per cent Marsanne.

CROZES-HERMITAGE	
Top Producers	**Other Recommended Producers**
Paul Jaboulet Aîné	Marcel Collange
Cave des Clairmonts	Chapoutier & Cie
(Borja)	Cave Coopérative des
Jules Fayolle	Vins Fins
Delas Frères	
Tardy & Ange	
J. & M. Ferraton	

St-Joseph

St-Joseph is the most recent of the northern Rhône appellations to gain *appellation contrôlée* status, which it did in 1956, twenty years after the others. The area is said to be named after the patron saint of betrayed husbands, though it is more likely to be derived from an ancient monastery that owned vineyards in the area. It is potentially by far the biggest northern appellation, though to date only about 350 hectares/865 acres are planted. The area under vines is expanding, however.

The St-Joseph vineyards start just south of Condrieu on the western bank of the Rhône, at Chavanay, and continue via the town of Tournon to Châteaubourg (just north of Cornas). The best vineyards are those with granitic soil on the hillsides overlooking the river between St-Jean-de-Muzols and Mauves, two villages situated north and south of Tournon. Here the hills rise fairly steeply from the river valley, with good drainage and favourable exposure to the sun. However, the small proportion of clay and sand in the soil and the slightly reduced exposure, compared with that enjoyed by the hill of Hermitage, result in a slightly less serious wine than Hermitage which is, therefore, cheaper. Elsewhere the ground is flatter, more fertile and less favourable for vine-growing. Tournon is peculiarly prone to thunderstorms; but while in the southern Rhône vineyards a thunderstorm can be catastrophic, here in the vineyards of St-Joseph the water runs quickly down the slopes. If a mistral wind follows the storm, as often happens, the vineyards dry out very rapidly so there is no serious risk of an epidemic of rot.

The St-Joseph appellation comprises seven communes; from north to south these are Chavanay, Vion, Lemps, St-Jean-de-Muzols, Tournon, Mauves and Glun. Of these only St-Jean-de-Muzols, Tournon and Mauves make fine wines, the other communes producing decidedly inferior wine. There has always been a friendly rivalry between the communities to the north of Tournon and those to the south, the northern winemakers taking a more rustic view of their profession. New plantations of vines are, sadly, not in the better locations; premium prices are paid for the best hillside land by developers from Valence for secluded residential areas. Hence the quality of St-Joseph wines varies according to their provenance, with the likelihood of a wine being less good as new plantings proceed.

St-Joseph produces predominantly red wine, though 20 per cent of the total production is white. The comparatively rare white is made from the Marsanne and Roussanne grapes. Formerly, red St-Joseph was made only with pure Syrah. However,

The vineyards of St-Joseph are less steep than those of Hermitage but still require terracing, which brings the attendant opportunities for advertising.

since 1980 it has been possible to include white grapes, up to a maximum of 10 per cent if the grapes are all fermented together. It is more likely that the alteration of the rules was made to make available greater quantities of the popular red wine than to improve its quality.

The red wines can never quite match the depth and concentration of Hermitage. They are likely to be lighter in body than most northern reds, except possibly certain wines from Crozes, but contain a surprisingly full bouquet, redolent of raspberries, blackberries and pepper. The wines can be expected to be well-coloured and fruity, but without the huge tannin or bitterness that is found in young Hermitage, Côte Rôtie and Cornas. Red St-Joseph should be drunk when it is between six and eight years old; only the great vintages last much longer.

Red wines are vinified in the same way as red Hermitage, although their lighter body means that they need no more than eighteen months in wood, though Jean Marsanne at Mauves occasionally gives his wines a little longer. He makes powerful, robust wine with plenty of spicy fruit, one of the fuller bodied wines from this appellation.

Pierre Coursodon also produces some of St-Joseph's best reds. He is based at Mauves, as is Gérard Chave, whose fine, elegant wines have a faithful following in Britain, though his production in only a tenth of that of M. Coursodon and is all red. Another of the most sought-after wines in the appellation is Jean-Louis Grippat's St-Joseph Cuvée des Hospices; only seventy-five to a hundred cases per year are made of this, though he also has a regular *cuvée* in larger quantities. His Cuvée des Hospices is one of the appellation's greatest red wines. Emile Florentin's Clos de l'Arbalestrier is another, though it can be hard and unyielding when young. Raymond Trollat, based at St-Jean-de-Muzols, makes rather more wine than Grippat from his vineyards on the top of a slope directly facing Hermitage across the river. His wine, too, is worth seeking out.

White wine is made by some but not all of the major producers. It can be excellent, full-bodied, with a delightful pear and apricot aroma. All too often, however, it is a little thin on flavour, hard and stalky. The wines are usually bottled young and are ready for drinking within a year following the harvest. They should not really be kept for longer than four years. Although good ones have been known to last for eight years or more, it is rarely worth taking the risk. Good producers of white wine include

ST-JOSEPH	
Top Producers	**Other Recommended Producers**
Gérard Chave	Delas Frères
Jean-Louis Grippat	E. Guigal
Raymond Trollat	(as Vidal-Fleury)
Pierre Coursodon	Bernard Gripa
Dr Emile Florentin	Paul Jaboulet Aîné
	Chapoutier & Cie

Bernard Gripa, who owns vineyards around Mauves, Jean-Louis Grippat and Raymond Trollat. Dr Florentin's whites are old-fashioned but good.

St-Joseph has its own cooperative, the *Cave Coopérative de St-Désirat-Champagne*. Two-thirds of the St-Joseph production, of wines of both colours, comes from this growers' cooperative. The quality of the wines is not outstanding and they are overshadowed by those from Tain's cooperative, which also offers St-Joseph.

CORNAS

Cornas produces some of the blackest wines that France can offer. They have been made since at least the end of the 9th century, when monks cultivated the vineyards and the Emperor Charlemagne halted his travels specially to sample the wine at Cornas. As well as their rich, intense colour, they have massive depth of fruit and tannin but, quite surprisingly, lack the staying power of a good quality Hermitage or Côte Rôtie.

Cornas marks the last red wine outpost of the northern Rhône. The flat valley below the vineyard slopes becomes wider as the river flows south towards the Mediterranean.

Cornas is a relatively small appellation, starting from the southern end of St-Joseph at Châteaubourg, encompassing the villages of Cornas and St-Péray, and finding its southern limits at the little village of Toulaud. Cornas is entirely situated on the west bank of the river. The appellation extends to 360 hectares/890 acres, but only about 60 are currently planted.

Cornas, like Côte Rôtie, makes only red wine. Not only are no white wines made, no white grapes are even planted (unlike Côte Rôtie) in spite of the fact that every year in December there is the annual Festival of the Syrah and the Roussette (a grape almost identical to Roussanne) in the village of Cornas. It must be assumed that Roussette is included in recognition of neighbouring St-Péray.

The older vineyards of Cornas are planted on the steep hillsides rising above the village. The village itself enjoys a warm, sunny situation, protected from the cold and violent winds by the semi-circular configuration of the hills behind. The village is set back from the river valley and so it is protected from the cold mistral wind. These slopes reach up to about 250 metres/275 yards in height and are often at a gradient of 45°, requiring stone-wall terracing. The microclimate of Cornas, combined with the heat-retaining qualities of the granitic soil, means that the vines receive more warmth than other appellations in the north, so the Syrah can ripen to achieve more colour and tannin than, for instance, in Hermitage which is seven miles to the north. Indeed, the very name of Cornas is derived from a Celtic word meaning scorched earth.

Granite and stones form the basis of the soil in Cornas, imparting quality to the wines as it does elsewhere in the northern Rhône appellations. However, some vineyards are also planted on the lighter, sandier ground at the foot of the slopes, known locally as the *sabot*, or boot. Here the land is flatter and accessible to tractors and other vineyard machinery, unlike the hillside sites which have to be worked by hand. The ever-expanding city of Valence constitutes a threat not only to the larger St-Joseph appellation but also to Cornas. New plantings of vines are increasingly confined to the less favourable, flat valley sites. There is no doubt but that these vineyards produce inferior wine, of less power and character, than those on the slopes.

Ignoring for the moment the diluting effect of the less well-sited vineyards, the potential of Cornas to produce huge, intense wines is brought about by three factors: its well-exposed situation, its unusual

(for the region) microclimate and the absence of any white grapes in the blend to temper the ferocity of well-ripened Syrah. Interestingly, Cornas is only allowed to produce a maximum yield of 35 hectolitres per hectare compared with 40 for some other northern red appellations, though, like St-Joseph, the wines are required to have a higher alcoholic strength, 10.5 degrees compared with 10 degrees for Côte Rôtie, Hermitage and Crozes-Hermitage.

Cornas has, when young, a four-square, masculine character, its fruit and possible finesse hidden beneath a solid layer of tannin and acidity. Theoretically it has all the promise of Hermitage, yet does not usually stay the course. Six to eight years should be allowed for the wine to mature, though its intense fruit can make it attractive when very young. In order to protect the fruit from drying out before the massive tannins soften up, the growers of Cornas now prefer to give their wine a slightly shorter *cuvaison*, five to six days in the vat instead of ten. This can produce a softer, rounder wine, although the traditional growers still like to give their wines eighteen months or more ageing in wood as well. Few people fine or filter their wines, so the black colour of young Cornas can be expected to appear as a big black sediment in later years; Cornas needs decanting to remove this, as well as to allow the wine to breathe and show at its best.

The best-known grower in Cornas is M. Auguste Clape, whose wines have become so sought-after at home and abroad that he never has enough to satisfy the demand, although he has increased his vineyard holdings over the years; he is now making about 2000 cases of Cornas each year. His wines are traditionally made, usually requiring the full six to eight years' keeping, depending on vintage, before they are ready to drink. He does not release them until they are two to three years old.

Another grower, Robert Michel, comes from a family with 400 years of winemaking tradition. His

CORNAS	
Top Producers	**Other Recommended Producers**
Auguste Clape	Marcel Juge
Noël Verset	Jean Lionnet
Robert Michel	Paul Jaboulet Aîné
Guy de Barjac	Chapoutier & Cie
	Delas Frères
	Cave Coopérative at Tain
	Alain Voge

wines are among the most robust and concentrated of anybody's, virtually all of the wine coming from the hillside vineyards.

Nearby are found the cellars of Guy de Barjac, who ferments his wine in contact with the skins for only six days, but then treats it as little as possible: no fining or filtration at all. His wines have plenty of fruit, flavour and body. It is his intention that the wine should show its true elegance before the fruit fades. His wine is frequently delicious at a very early stage.

Noël Verset makes excellent wine with great concentration and depth from some of the best situated vines in the appellation. His wine is of the old school and needs long keeping, but also offers longevity once the wine is mature.

Of the *négociants*, Chapoutier, Jaboulet and Delas Frères all offer a respectable, sometimes excellent, Cornas, and I have always enjoyed the offerings from Tain's *cave coopérative*.

ST-PÉRAY

St-Péray is the most southerly of the northern Rhône vineyards, adjacent to those of Cornas. The village of St-Péray is tiny but carries a mention in Michelin's guides as the gateway to the Corniche de l'Eyrieux, which offers a splendid tour of the hills of the Vivarais behind St-Péray. Also, 200 metres/218 yards above the valley are the ruins of the Château de Crussol, billed as one of the more grandiose sites in the Rhône valley, affording a fabulous view over Valence and the Rhône river.

In times gone by, St-Péray enjoyed great fame and fortune. Napoleon Bonaparte attributed his first discovery of wine to St-Péray and legend also has it that Richard Wagner, while in the middle of composing *Parsifal*, sent off for a hundred inspiring bottles to be delivered to Bayreuth.

Nowadays St-Péray is little known for its wines, all of which are white. Eighty per cent of the production is made as a *méthode champenoise* sparkling wine, the rest as a still dry wine. No Viognier is planted here, only Marsanne and the Roussanne. There is also the Roussette, so similar to Roussanne as to make the distinction academic. In any case, the Marsanne comprises four-fifths of the plantations.

The appellation of St-Péray comprises a variety of soil types but contains no chalk, unlike in Champagne. As a result of this, and the vastly warmer climate enjoyed by St-Péray, the base wine is less acid, so the wines can never closely resemble those of Champagne, although the method of production is virtually identical.

For sparkling wine a degree of acidity is necessary to give the required bite and freshness. It is vital, therefore, that in the warm climes of St-Péray the grapes are not allowed to overripen. Normally they are picked relatively early, at the beginning of October. Grapes for the still wine are left a week or so longer as the extra acid is not desirable.

The still wine of St-Péray is vinified like all the other northern Rhône whites, with some ageing in wood. This can result in heavy wines, rather prone to oxidation, although the better ones have enough backbone and flesh to survive up to ten years in bottle. Normally St-Péray should be drunk up after half this time, and will seldom be more than a solid, fat, heavy wine with nutty, peachy fruit at its best (or tiredness at its worst), without much green acidity except in lean years. With age the wine will deepen in colour and develop a creamy character.

The sparkling wines rarely, but occasionally, bear a vintage, normally being sold as a non-vintage blend. Sparkling St-Péray is rather heavier and coarser than champagne, more Spanish or southern in style, but good examples can show off the flowery, pear-like scents of the Marsanne and Roussanne.

Few growers are to be found in St-Péray; 75 per cent of the wine is made by the *Cave des Vignerons de St-Péray*. Producers from Cornas, such as Auguste Clape, Alain Voge, Marcel Juge and Jean Teysseire also make some St-Péray, though usually as a sideline to their output of Cornas. Of the merchants in the village, the best-known are Eugène Verilhac and Gilles Père & Fils, both of whom buy in most of their grapes.

The better known growers include Jean-François Chaboud and Pierre Darona, both of whom make predominantly sparkling wines. Chaboud does make a vintage sparkler as well as a non-vintage blend, and both make a little still wine. Michel Milliand, another well-respected grower, has 7 hectares/17 acres of vines fragmented across the whole of the appellation, so that he can produce a consistent blend more easily by careful selection of his grapes. Of the *négociants*, Delas Frères produce a still St-Péray that is a most respectable example.

ST-PÉRAY	
Leading Producers	
Caves des Vignerons de St-Péray	Pierre Darona
	Jean Teysseire
Jean-François Chaboud	Delas Frères

It is easy to follow a tour of the northern Rhône vineyards by another in the south but as the two regions are physically separate there is no reason why the southern tour should not be saved up for a different occasion if time is limiting.

CHÂTEAUNEUF-DU-PAPE

Châteauneuf-du-Pape is a name familiar even to those who may not be specially well versed in wine lore; along with St Emilion and Nuits-St Georges, Châteauneuf-du-Pape used to convey the idea of a style rather than a particular origin.

Châteauneuf-du-Pape achieved fame at the beginning of the fourteenth century when Pope Clement V planted a vineyard, later extended by Pope John XXII. This proved insufficient to supply the demands of the papal palace so other growers were encouraged to offer their wines as well.

The first Châteauneuf wine to be sold in bottle was Château La Nerthe is 1785, followed in 1815 by Domaine de la Solitude. La Nerthe was the most highly regarded and exported wine in Châteauneuf until the second half of the nineteenth century. At that time the wine was not even called Châteauneuf-du-Pape, but Châteauneuf-Calcernies, after the limestone quarries near the village.

The fortunes of Châteauneuf-du-Pape declined after phylloxera struck in the late nineteenth century and demand for the wine subsided. The next, and very important, milestone in its history came in 1923, when Baron Le Roy of Château Fortia, one of the best estates in the area, put forward a charter stipulating six criteria to be obeyed for the production of Châteauneuf. These were as follows:

(1) The wines had to be produced from a precisely delimited area.
(2) Only specific grape varieties could be grown within the area.
(3) The cultivation techniques for the vines were to be controlled.
(4) The wine had to contain a minimum 12.5 degrees alcohol.
(5) At harvest time, 5 per cent of the crop had to be discarded (*triage*) to ensure the inclusion only of healthy, well-ripened grapes.

(6) No rosé wine was to be made, and only wines that passed a tasting panel would be allowed to bear the name Châteauneuf-du-Pape.

These rules represented the starting point for the entire French *appellation contrôlée* system, which was adopted in 1936, and they essentially still control the production of Châteauneuf-du-Pape today. In 1954 two further articles were attached to the six laws to the effect that no flying saucer would be allowed within the commune of Châteauneuf-du-Pape, and any that landed there would immediately be taken off to the pound! Not a great threat today but these articles indicate how seriously the new laws were taken.

The delineated area of Châteauneuf is currently almost fully planted and covers about 3150 hectares/7785 acres under vines. The vineyards form a rough circle with the town in the centre, all to the east of the Rhône. The southernmost part of the appellation starts less than seven miles north of Avignon, and finishes another eight miles or so further north, just south of Orange and Jonquières. The terrain is hilly, with a gently rising plateau north of the village, and undulating ground to the south, east and west.

Part of the vineyard area is covered with large cream and rust-coloured stones, alluvial deposits left by retreating Alpine glaciers thousands of years ago. The greatest covering of stones lies in the vineyards to the north and north-west of the village in the Domaines de Mont-Redon and Les Cabrières, where virtually no soil can be seen underneath these large pebbles. The same is true of Vieux Télégraphe in the east. Areas to the south are more gravelly, whereas those to the east are generally less stony, with clay and sand in the subsoil. These areas produce wines that are a little lighter in alcoholic content than those grown in the stoniest parts.

Châteauneuf-du-Pape produces mainly red wines; about 4 per cent of the total is white. No rosé is allowed. Thirteen different grape varieties are permitted, but only eight of these are red. White grapes are often included in the red wine blend as they each add their own particular qualities. The main red grapes are the Grenache, Syrah, Cinsault and Mourvèdre with the Terret Noir, Muscardin, Vaccarèse and Counoise also being authorized. The white grapes allowed do not, oddly, include the white Grenache, permitted elsewhere in the Rhône valley, but instead comprise Clairette, Bourboulenc, Roussanne, Picpoul and Picardin. Most Châteauneuf-du-Pape producers stick to just a few of the thirteen grapes; the most widely planted is Grenache. Château Rayas makes its red Châteauneuf from almost 100 per cent Grenache, whereas Domaine de Beaucastel, Domaine Mont-Redon and Domaine de Nalys actually use all thirteen varieties, though this is unusual. Local opinion varies as to the value of in-

dividual grape varieties. François Perrin of Domaine de Beaucastel is not enamoured of the Cinsault, preferring the lesser-known Counoise, yet has both planted in his estate. He also has a strong belief in the Mourvèdre as a grape with a great future.

Last century a certain Commandant Duclos made known what he considered were the contents of his ideal vat: 20 per cent Grenache and Cinsault, to provide the wine with 'warmth, liqueur-like sweetness and mellowness', 40 per cent Mourvèdre, Syrah, Muscardin and Vaccarèse, to give it 'solidity, durability and colour, accompanied by a straightfor-

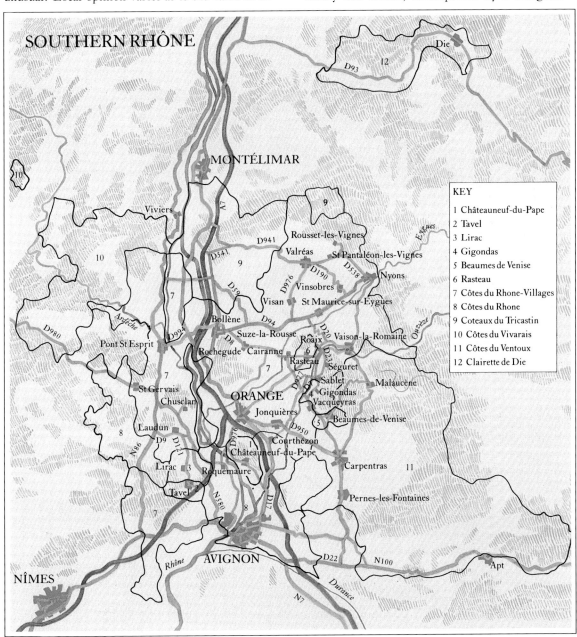

SOUTHERN RHÔNE

KEY
1 Châteauneuf-du-Pape
2 Tavel
3 Lirac
4 Gigondas
5 Beaumes de Venise
6 Rasteau
7 Côtes du Rhone-Villages
8 Côtes du Rhone
9 Coteaux du Tricastin
10 Côtes du Vivarais
11 Côtes du Ventoux
12 Clairette de Die

*'Sur le pont d'Avignon, on y danse, tout en rond'. Nowadays this bridge at Avignon
is more of a sightseeing spot than a venue for dancing.*

ward, almost thirst-quenching flavour'; 30 per cent
Counoise and Picpoul, to supply 'vinosity, charm,
freshness and accentuation of bouquet' and 10 per
cent Clairette and Bourboulenc to bring 'finesse, fire
and sparkle' to the wine. Commandant Duclos did
not recommend all thirteen grape varieties, in keeping with most Châteauneuf estates' practices but,
even so, most producers nowadays use 60–75 per
cent Grenache to boost the alcohol, with an increasing amount of the flavoursome Syrah, at the expense
of the lesser known varieties.

The cultivation techniques for Châteauneuf-du-
Pape are controlled by Baron Le Roy's rules, which
are mainly common sense. Every year during the
vintage the grapes (picked separately by variety) are
sorted to reject 5 per cent at least (the *triage*). In
theory, this means that all unripe and rotten grapes
will be discarded, but, in practice, it is difficult to
supervise the *triage* everywhere, so it is by no means
certain that it will be thoroughly carried out, if at all,
though estates that pride themselves on their good

reputation can be relied upon to do so.

Châteauneuf-du-Pape's red wine can vary enormously in style and quality, not just because of the
possible combinations of the thirteen grape varieties
and the variations in soil across the region, but also
because of the different methods of vinification
employed. The classic method involves a long
maceration of the grape must with the skins at comparatively high temperatures to produce robust,
highly coloured, tannic, long-lasting wines. Such
methods are used at some of the best known estates:
Les Clefs d'Or, Domaine de Beaucastel and Clos du
Mont-Olivet, although at Beaucastel the partially
crushed grapes are heated to 90°C/194°F to kill off
wild yeasts before cooling. Cultured yeasts are then
added and the fermentation proceeds normally.

The carbonic semi-maceration method practised
in Beaujolais and in parts of the southern Rhône valley is also used in Châteauneuf-du-Pape, at Domaine
de la Solitude and Domaine de Nalys for example.
However, the majority of producers use a com-

Château les Fines Roches in Châteauneuf-du-Pape is one of the more imposing buildings in the area.

bination of both methods: traditional fermentation for Syrah, Mourvèdre and part of the Grenache crop, with the other half of the harvest (mainly Grenache and Cinsault) vinified from uncrushed grapes or by carbonic maceration. This method, practised by estates such as Domaine de Beauregard and Domaine de Mont-Redon, allows the wine to have some fresh fruit and mellowness, yet retaining enough body, tannin and structure to ensure it will keep for a few years. Many of the better estates will age their wine in wooden barrels before bottling.

It is difficult to describe accurately the aroma and flavours of red Châteauneuf-du-Pape. Unlike Hermitage or Côte Rôtie, there are no obvious varietal characteristics. The best wines are rich, robust and herby, with flavours of ripe fruits and roasted meat or game, smoky, leathery aromas and peppery overtones. The alcoholic content is always striking; the legal minimum of 12.5 degrees is the highest in France and it is not unknown for wines to reach 14 degrees or more. Red Châteauneuf-du-Pape will

take four to five years to mature on average and have a lifetime of about eight to ten years – although the best wines of exceptional vintages can easily last for twenty.

The little white wine made at Châteauneuf-du-Pape can be rich and flavoursome but is often heavy and dull. Good ones include the Domaine de Nalys, Clos de l'Oratoire de Papes, Château Rayas and Domaine du Vieux Télégraphe. On the whole, white Châteauneuf is best drunk young.

About a quarter of the total production of Châteauneuf-du-Pape is estate-bottled. These wines are allowed to be bottled in the distinctive, heavy, old-style bottles showing the Papal coat of arms and the words Châteauneuf-du-Pape embossed in the glass. Other bottles that can be seen include the twisted La Fiole, used sometimes by the *négociant* firm Père Anselme, and specially designed ones used by Château Rayas and Château La Gardine.

There are two separate growers' associations as well as individual estates and domaines. The first,

Prestige & Tradition, comprises ten growers who share bottling and warehousing facilities (a kind of mini-cooperative) including the illustrious name of Domaine de la Solitude. This domaine also forms part of the second association, Les Reflets, founded in 1954 and led by three well-known domaines: Les Cailloux, Chante-Perdrix and Clos du Mont-Olivet. Both associations produce wines that are among the best that the appellation has to offer.

There is just one *cave coopérative* at Châteauneuf-du-Pape, *Le Cellier des Princes* at Courthézon, which produces acceptable reds that mature rapidly, as they contain a high proportion of Grenache.

Of the individual properties, there is no official rating of vineyards as there is in Bordeaux, although some produce consistently better wine that others. One of my favourite estates is the Domaine du Vieux Télégraphe, owned by Henri Brunier. His wine is vinified in new stainless steel, although it is later put in cement vats to encourage the malolactic fermentation and finally into oak casks to mature for a year. Vieux Télégraphe red is predominantly comprised of Grenache, and because the vines are, on average, over forty years old, they yield rich, deep, concentrated wines totally different to the dilute 'strawberry-jam' Côtes du Rhône type that comes from younger vines. Syrah, Mourvèdre and Cinsault provide the remaining 30 per cent of the crop, so the overall result is a well-structured, profound wine. Modern vinification allows the wine to be supple and charming rather than solid and heavy. When mature (three to ten years old) M. Brunier's wines are elegant, finely balanced and oozing with flavour.

The Domaine de Beaucastel also makes consistently excellent wine, although the style is different from that of Vieux Télégraphe. To start with, M. Perrin plants all thirteen grape varieties compared to Brunier's four, with a relatively high proportion (30 per cent) of Mourvèdre. Beaucastel is the longest lived red wine of Châteauneuf-du-Pape; it has enormous depth of colour and aroma, as well as sheer power and tannin. It is a more solid wine than Vieux Télégraphe, with the fruit taking longer to show above the tannin. The wine is not filtered, to preserve all its aromas and nuances, but clarified by fining with egg whites. It does, therefore, give a heavy deposit in the bottle. There is also a little white Beaucastel made here; unlike other white Châteauneufs it does have ageing potential.

The third top-flight Châteauneuf-du-Pape comes from Château Rayas. The red wine is unusual in that it is made almost entirely from the Grenache grape,

though from low yielding, carefully tended vines of fifty-five to seventy years of age. As at Vieux Télégraphe this gives a rich, concentrated wine of great intensity with opulence, and its staying power almost compares with that of Beaucastel. In some years all or part of the crop is declassified and sold under a secondary label, Château Pignan, which can offer exceptional value as Rayas is the most expensive wine in Châteauneuf-du-Pape. There is also a Rayas white wine made in tiny quantities.

One of the three leading domaines, Vieux Télégraphe is the more feminine in style than the other two, and certainly more charming in its youth. Beaucastel offers greater complexity than Rayas due to the inclusion of Syrah, Mourvèdre and Cinsault though they both show well on the grounds of supreme concentration. It also, like Vieux Télégraphe, drinks well when young.

There are also a number of other domaines producing good quality Châteauneuf-du-Pape. Other recommended producers are included in the list below. Worthy of special mention, however, are Château La Nerthe and Domaine Mont-Redon.

Château La Nerthe, sitting splendidly on a small rise to the south-east of the village, is the most famous estate historically. The house itself is still undergoing extensive refurbishment since its purchase in 1985 by the firm of *négociants*, David & Foillard, who are also increasing the area planted with vines. A regular *cuvée*, powerful, solid and fruity, is available along with a special 'Vieilles Vignes', Cuvée Les Cadettes, which is full of fruit and concentration. New oak barrels have been introduced on an experimental basis at this estate.

The biggest estate in Châteauneuf-du-Pape is that of Domaine Mont-Redon, whose 130 hectares/320 acres is about the same size as the whole of Côte Rôtie. The red wines are good, not too heavy, as they have lightened the style in recent years, and are of consistent quality, while their white wine production (4,500 cases) is larger than anyone else's. A small quantity of distilled grape brandy, Marc de Châteauneuf-du-Pape, is made here and sold privately.

Sadly, there is also some dreadful wine made in Châteauneuf-du-Pape, which rides on the good reputation of the majority. Most of the culprits are the big *négociants* (including those from Burgundy who have some Rhône wines in their portfolio) whose desire to offer large quantities leads to reductions in quality. The *négociants* listed can be relied upon to produce typical and acceptable wine, though not of the same class (or price bracket) as the good estates.

*The town of Châteauneuf-du-Pape is dominated by the ruins of the castle
built by Pope John XXII, almost completely destroyed during World War II.*

CHÂTEAUNEUF-DU-PAPE		
Top Producers	**Other Recommended Producers**	***Négociants* and *Coopératives***
Château Rayas Domaine de Beaucastel Domaine du Vieux Télégraphe	Domaine de Mont-Redon Château de la Nerthe Domaine de Beaurenard Domaine Chante-Cigale Les Clefs d'Or Clos de l'Oratoire des Papes Clos des Papes Clos du Mont-Olivet Château Fortia Cuvée du Vatican Domaine de Nalys Domaine de la Solitude Château des Fines-Roches Château de la Gardine Prestige & Tradition Les Reflets	Le Cellier des Princes Caves St-Pierre Caves Bessac Delas Frères E. Guigal P. Jaboulet Aîné

TAVEL

'*Le Premier Vin Rosé de France*' proclaim the signs proudly on all sides as you enter the village of Tavel. Whether or not you happen to agree will depend partly on whether you like your pink wine to be sweet or dry. Tavel's rosé is always dry; and is certainly one of the best in France. The *appellation contrôlée* is only for rosé wine; red and white wines from here are sold as either Lirac or Côtes du Rhône.

Tavel first achieved fame in the thirteenth century when King Philip Le Bel decided that it was the only source of good wine in the country, though it is sad to think that he might have missed other Rhône wines.

Tavel thrived in the eighteenth and nineteenth centuries. The wine was shipped overseas, where its aged characteristics from maturation en route were much appreciated. Even today, many think of Tavel as a wine that keeps well, though it is really better drunk while young and is not intended for laying down.

Tavel is situated in the Gard *département* between Orange and Avignon, but well west of both. The A9 motorway passes within yards of the village although it has no exit here. Tavel is marked by striking scenery, or, some might say, the lack of it. Here are arid *garrigues*, rocky hillocks and dried-out vegetation; chalky cliffs lie to the west of the village overlooking the Vallongue plateau to the north.

Other villages in the south also produce rosé though not of the same quality. What makes Tavel different is mainly the soil in its vineyards. To look at, the soil appears very similar to parts of Châteauneuf-du-Pape; the ground is covered with those same cream and rust-coloured stones which retain the sun's heat so well. These stones come from the same alluvial deposits that are in Châteauneuf, yet underneath all is different. Tavel has sand and chalk, which is less suitable for red wine than the gravel, clay and limestone of Châteauneuf. Sand and chalk make lighter wines, and so are much more suitable for rosé

TAVEL	
Recommended Producers	
Cave Coopérative des Grands Crus de Tavel	M. Roudil (Le Vieux Moulin de Tavel)
M. Méjan-Taulier (Clos Canto-Perdrix)	M. Olivier (Château d'Aquéria)
M. Maby (Domaine de la Forcadière)	M. Lafond (Domaine Corne-Loup)
Mme. Bernard (Domaine de la Genestière)	

than red. Vines are planted both on the slopes and on the Vallongue plateau.

Today there are approximately 750 hectares/1853 acres of vineyards, as there have been since the early nineteenth century. Nine different grape varieties can be planted. Of the red grapes, the alcohol-giving Grenache cannot exceed 60 per cent of the total, while the tempering effect of the Cinsault must be included to at least 15 per cent. The coarse Carignan is limited to 10 per cent or less, while the more noble red grapes of Syrah and Mourvèdre have only been allowed since 1969. Calitor, the sixth red grape, is now being phased out. The white grapes permitted comprise Clairette, Picpoul and Bourboulenc.

The rosé wine is made by allowing the red grape skins only twenty-four to forty-eight hours at the most in contact with the grape must. Even then, Tavel is one of the most highly coloured, dark rosés to be found. Freshness in the wine is of paramount importance, so the better producers use stainless steel vats to keep the must cool. Whole grapes are put in the vats and their weight causes a little crushing ; thus the fermentation begins slowly and can be more easily controlled. It lasts just a week on average. The wine is always fermented to dryness. Not all growers permit the malolactic fermentation to proceed, as some prefer to keep the higher acidity and bite in their wine by preventing this process. The wine is bottled early, in the spring following the vintage.

Tavel can easily reach 13 or 14 degrees alcohol, which can upset the balance of the wine. It is for this reason that the proportion of Grenache is limited. Young Tavel should be fresh, vibrant and stimulating, with an aroma of strawberries and a long, satisfying finish. The depth of flavour tempts many to keep the wine for a few years expecting it to develop; however, usually it becomes coarse and clumsy once the fresh fruit character fades.

Over half the wine from Tavel is made at the village cooperative. There are a few private domaines, otherwise the grapes are bought up by *négociants* to complete their range of Rhône wines.

LIRAC

Lirac is rather the Cinderella of the Rhône valley. Although it has had full *appellation contrôlée* status since 1945, and has tripled its area under vines to over 600 hectares/1480 acres since then, few have heard of it or appreciate the fine quality of the wines.

Lirac has two historical claims to fame, only one of which is honourable. This is that the four villages which today make up the Lirac appellation were

*Tavel's vines are carefully trained on wires to facilitate picking and
circulation of air. The trees help break the force of the mistral wind in this vineyard.
The vines are planted in rows wide apart to permit the passage of vineyard machinery.*

among the first to be recognized officially as producers of Côtes du Rhône, along with Tavel, Orsan, Chusclan and Codolet. Wine from these villages was entitled to have the letters CdR (for Côtes du Rhône) branded on the barrels. So began an official classification around Lirac, but so also began something far less welcome 136 years later in 1867. The owner of Château de Clary at Lirac, whose domaine still remains, decided to experiment with his vines and imported new varieties from abroad. The American vines he planted carried the phylloxera lice in their roots, which infected not only the de Clary vineyard but, soon after, spread across Europe, destroying all the European vines in their wake.

Lirac lies close to Tavel on a tiny road about 3 kilometres/2 miles west of Roquemaure. The appellation covers three other villages, as Lirac itself is so small. These are Roquemaure, St-Laurent-des-Arbres and St-Géniès-de-Comolas, none of which is much bigger.

Although Lirac is so close to Tavel, the soil in the vineyards is very different. The hillsides are gently sloping and their gravel soil drains well. At Roquemaure is a stony plateau, containing big stones similar to those in Châteauneuf-du-Pape, whose vineyards are only a short distance away on the other side of the river. The slopes are well exposed, the hot, dry climate is favourable and the grapes ripen easily.

Lirac produces mainly red wines, as well as some white and rosé. The latter can be extremely good on occasions. As in Tavel, Grenache is the predominant grape variety (limited to 60 per cent maximum), although Cinsault also features strongly. Other grapes include Calitor and Carignan (restricted to a maximum of 10 per cent), Ugni blanc, Clairette, Bourboulenc, Picpoul and Maccabéo. Vintaging starts towards mid-September for white grapes, and a little later for the red ones.

The grapes are vinified by the semi-maceration

technique that is used in Tavel. White and rosé wines are bottled early, to retain freshness. Most red wine is also bottled young, though occasionally it is matured for a time. At Château St-Roch, perhaps the best Lirac domaine, the wine is aged for a year in tanks and then for at least six months in big wooden vats before bottling.

Red Lirac is generally light and fruity, often lighter in body than Côtes du Rhône-Villages wines from the Vaucluse *département*, but still of excellent quality. Its rich, herby, plummy characteristics balance well and make a delightful wine, which can be drunk up to its fourth birthday, as a rule. Often the wines offer remarkable value as they are 'forgotten' by those willing to pay far higher prices for Gigondas or Châteauneuf-du-Pape.

In addition to the cooperatives at Roquemaure and St-Laurent-des-Arbres, there are a number of individual domaines; Antoine Verda's Domaine du Château St-Roch is the highest regarded, although the old-established Château de Clary and Château de Ségriès also produce lovely wine. A delightful story surrounds Castel Oualou, established in 1961. The name actually means 'there is no castle', which there isn't, so the wine label shows a picture of the castle in *Snow White and the Seven Dwarfs*. When the official name inspectors came to investigate, they did not share the proprietor's sense of humour and insisted that a cross was printed over the castle, which the label still shows today. There may not be a castle, but there is plenty of wine which can be delicious.

André Méjan at Domaine Méjan makes one of the biggest bodied wines in Lirac. His Les Queyrades is a plump, rounded wine, tannic when young, generously fruity when mature.

M. Maby's Domaine la Fermade is one of the better known names for Lirac and Tavel in the UK. He makes a delicious, fresh white wine and a deep-coloured, highly scented, quite powerful red.

GIGONDAS

Gigondas is the latest addition to the list of full *appellation contrôlée* wines in the Rhône valley, though it will not necessarily be the last. It achieved this status in 1971 for its red and rosé wines. White wine is also made here, though it can only be sold as Côtes du Rhône. The town, or rather village, of Gigondas is small, but picturesque. It nestles among low hills against the backdrop of the Dentelles de Montmirail.

The vineyard areas of Gigondas are spread out over a variety of locations, and the area under vines has been extended and restructured since 1971, not

LIRAC	
Recommended Producers	
M. Verda (Domaine du Château St-Roch)	Mme. Pons-Mure (Castel Oualou)
M. de Régis (Château de Ségriès)	M. Lombardo (Domaine du Devoy)
M. Maby (Domaine la Fermade)	M. Pons-Mure (Domaine de la Tour de Lirac)
M. Mayer (Château de Clary)	M. Méjan (Domaine Méjan)

*These gently sloping vineyards above the village of Gigondas are
of sufficient altitude to counteract the richness of the clay soil.*

always in aspects that receive the most warmth and sunshine. Since the Second World War, the area under vines has increased at least three-fold. The highest vineyards (up to 600 metres/1968ft) are planted on the steepest slopes of the lower reaches of the Dentelles de Montmirail. Here the soil is a rich, yellowish clay. If the richness of the soil were not balanced by the height of the vineyards, the Grenache, naturally a grape that gives alcoholic wines, would make too heavy a wine.

Descending towards the Ouvèze valley, the slopes flatten out a little and the ground becomes stonier, with concomitant better drainage and more suitable, poorer soils. These are among the best sites that Gigondas can offer: Grenache, Syrah, Cinsault, Mourvèdre and the white Clairette are all planted here. Further down still, on the sandy and stony plain surrounding the river Ouvèze, the more robust, earthy style wines are produced.

Wine has been made at Gigondas since Roman times; indeed the name of the village is reputed to derive from the Latin *jocunditas* meaning 'merry

city'. From the 9th century the nuns at the Abbey of St-André were believed to have made wine, and later the abbey became home to the Bishops of Orange, displaced from Avignon by the Popes. As time went on, Gigondas began to be appreciated elsewhere in France and was used extensively to fortify burgundy, just as Hermitage found a home in Bordeaux blends. Even so it was not regarded seriously in its own right. It was just a component of Côtes du Rhône.

After the Second World War, Gigondas' two *négociant* companies, Amadieu and Meffre, were formed and the local *vignerons* began to take more pride in their wine. The mediocre Carignan grape was banned from the region, and Gigondas adopted the practice of *triage*, already well-established in Châteauneuf-du-Pape. Interestingly enough, the *appellation contrôlée* laws make no stricter requirements for yield (35 hectolitres per hectare) or minimum alcoholic degree (12.5) than for Côtes du Rhône-Villages from which Gigondas was promoted. However, it is not unusual for the wine to achieve 13–14.5 degrees alcohol to rival the heady qualities of Châteauneuf-du-Pape. No more that 80 per cent of the wine can be Grenache, and no less than 15 per cent Syrah.

The vineyard ownership in Gigondas is dominated by the *négociants* Amadieu and Meffre, the latter owning more *appellation contrôlée* vineyards in terms of area under vines than anyone else in France. There are also, however, a number of much smaller domaines, often much older than those owned by the *négociants*; for example, relics of Roman drinking vessels have been discovered at the Domaine Raspail-Ay. Naturally Gigondas has its own *cave coopérative* to cater for the growers with only small holdings or no equipment. It makes a fruity, round Gigondas that has the distinction of being the house wine of the Michelin 3-starred restaurant, L'Oustau de Baumanière, at Les Baux in Provence.

The making of the wine at Gigondas can be both traditional or modern, or possibly a combination of both. Some domaines, such as Domaine Les Pallières, will age their wine in wood for up to three years afterwards. The other extreme involves the *macération carbonique* methods practised for Côtes du Rhône, to give a well-coloured but faster maturing wine.

Even so, Gigondas is frequently a deep-coloured wine, purple-black when young, with a dizzy degree of alcohol and rustic aromas of thyme, pepper, roasted meat and blackberries. Some wines are full of tannin, although Gigondas is rarely a hard, astringent wine; rather it tends to be full and supple. The style and qualities of the wines vary considerably. At the top end Jean-Pierre Cartier's Florence at Domaine Les Goubert is a well-structured, rich, fragrant and herbal wine without being overpowering or 'cooked', whereas that from Domaine Raspail-Ay is more intense and heavy, a Châteauneuf 'lookalike'. The better wines are characterized by sufficient acidity to balance the alcohol; Roger Combe's L'Oustau Fauquet succeeds admirably on this front.

Roger Meffre at Domaine St-Gayan obtains intensity of flavour from having older vines in his vineyard. The rich, smoky, gamey style is also found in the Roux brothers' Domaine Les Pallières. However, at the other end of the scale, Gigondas can be too alcoholic and 'cooked' with insufficient depth or fruit to balance: the *négociant* wines can often be criticized for this fault, while even Paul Jaboulet's recent Gigondas offerings suffer slightly in the same way.

BEAUMES-DE-VENISE

This small Roman village that nestles below the Dentelles de Montmirail is one of the seventeen specified Côtes du Rhône-Villages, yet also has full *appellation contrôlée* status for its spicy, scented dessert Muscat wine that is different in style from Muscat wine produced anywhere else.

The popularity of Muscat de Beaumes-de-Venise has increased dramatically in recent years, resulting in a greater area of Muscat plantations. These now cover 230 hectares/568 acres; in 1945 when the *appellation contrôlée* was granted, there were only 40 hectares/98 acres.

The Muscat grape is the Muscat *à petit grains* variety, elsewhere known as the Muscat d'Alexandria. It has two sub-varieties: the Grain blanc and the Grain noir. Both are needed to obtain the right, pale orange colour in the wine. It is not an easy grape to cultivate, falling prey to diseases such as grey rot and oidium and pests like the red spider. Muscat grapes ripen fast, but are usually left on the vine as late as mid-October to have as much sugar as possible (so that less alcohol – which is expensive – will need to be added). A description of how the wines are actually made and fortified is given on page 24.

Traditionally the Muscat was made of a strength similar to port or sherry; that is to say between 17 and 21 degrees alcohol. Now 15.5 degrees is the norm, offered by the huge *cave coopérative* that produces 90 per cent of all the Muscat made. M. Nativelle at the excellent Domaine de Coyeux, however, has recognized that Great Britain is an important market for his wine, and makes it at 15 degrees exactly, so that it attracts a lower rate of excise duty than the higher strength wines.

Muscat de Beaumes-de-Venise is pale orangey-gold in colour, with an opulent, intense aroma of ripe Muscat grapes and spicy, oriental fruits. It is enormously rich and sweet with a powerful aftertaste. Traditionally the Muscat is served as a dessert, or after-dinner, wine (it is one of the few wines that can cope with chocolate) but is also good with a starter of

GIGONDAS	
Leading Producers	
Pierre Amadieu	Jean-Pierre Cartier
Gabriel Meffre	(Domaine Les Goubert)
Roger Meffre (Domaine	François Ay (Domaine
St-Gayan)	Raspail-Ay)
Serge Chapalain (Domaine	Cave Coopérative
de Longue-Toque)	Roger Combe (Domaine
Hilarion Roux (Les Fils	L'Oustau Fauquet)
de Les Pallières)	Michel Feraud

*In the shadows of the Dentelles de Montmirail lies the quiet village
of Beaumes de Venise. Village life centres round the cafés where one can
always enjoy a reviving glass of sweet Muscat or red Côtes du Rhône-Villages.*

melons or with ice as an aperitif. The *cave coopérative* recognizes not only its versatility but also its ability to keep well once opened, so they bottle the wine in a clear glass, fancy embossed bottle, not unlike a large scent bottle, with a screw cap so the wine can be consumed over several days. The domaine-owners usually use a clear, flute-shaped bottle with a driven cork, which conveys an image of higher quality.

There are, however, very few estate-bottled Muscats. The Domaine Durban and Domaine de Coyeux are the best known, while Jean-Pierre Perrin at La Vieille Ferme (making Côtes du Ventoux) makes a little; so does Guy Rey (another Ventoux producer). The last estate is the Domaine des Bernardins. Of the *négociants* Vidal-Fleury (now owned by the house of Guigal) has an excellent offering.

RASTEAU

If Beaumes-de-Venise is unusual among the Côtes du Rhône-Villages, then so is Rasteau for its Grenache-based dessert wines. These *Vins Doux Naturels* are the only wines of the village which are entitled to the full *Appellation Rasteau Contrôlée*. Nevertheless there are no defined vineyard sites for them, since Grenache may also be used for the red Côtes du Rhône-Villages. In practice, however, there is a division of sites as the best, ripest grapes reserved for the sweet wine come from the chalky-clay slopes rather than on the plains below the village. It is also believed that older vines are better producers for dessert wine as their grapes contain more sugar.

As the laws stipulate that grapes for the *Vin Doux Naturel* must have at least the equivalent of 15 degrees alcohol in sugar at the time of picking, little is made in poor years. The grapes are harvested in mid-October.

There are three styles of the *Vin Doux Naturel*. The traditional red wine is vinified with the grape skins to provide the colour and backbone of the wine. It is, however, a taste for purists and only accounts for 7 per cent of the total dessert wine produced. The growers and connoisseurs love it but admit that its heavy, sometimes tannic, style is much less commercial than the golden, *'dorée'*, style which is vinified away from the grape skins to keep the colour light, although it is in fact a dark yellow, gold colour. The golden version is more obviously sweet with a honeyed, caramelized character, whereas the red has more fruit and a touch of bitterness. Both wines will have had a year or two's ageing in cask, but there is a third style of wine that has spent much longer in wood. This style is reminiscent of old tawny port (also made by long maturation in wood), but, in addition, has a strange, slightly oxidized, rancid, bitter flavour. This *'rancio'* style is much prized by the producers and tastes considerably better than it sounds, as well as having an attractive, mellow roundness absent from the other wines. It is, however, considered an acquired taste.

Only the cooperative produces any of the red *Vin Doux*, of which it is justly proud while admitting that its red Côtes du Rhône-Villages table wines are what keeps its coffers full. A few growers also make dessert wine at their domaines, but again as a sideline to accompany the dry red.

Although the sweet wine is something of a curiosity, the cooperative at Rasteau claim that there is a healthy demand for these wines within France, and sales are keeping pace with production. The wines are hardly known at all within the UK, but can be recommended for drinking either as an aperitif (which is how they are usually treated in France) or as a change from port or Madeira after dinner.

These vines above Rasteau are of sufficient age to produce only a small yield and, therefore, better quality wine is made than from young vines.

CÔTES DU RHÔNE-VILLAGES

In 1967 the authorities responsible for *appellation contrôlée*, the INAO (Institut National d'Appellations d'Origine) decided that seventeen villages within the Côtes du Rhône area were worthy of special distinction as their vineyards had superior soils, aspects and climate to those making ordinary Côtes du Rhône. These villages were not, however, judged worthy of full *appellation contrôlée* status in their own right. Each village can sell its wine under the appellation Côtes du Rhône-Villages, or the label may bear the village name, with the words Côtes du Rhône in front of it. A blend of two or more of these villages can be sold as plain Côtes du Rhône-Villages. Not all seventeen villages were granted this privilege at first; in 1953 there were just four: Cairanne, Chusclan, Laudun and Gigondas, of which Gigondas was promoted to its own appellation in 1971.

In addition to the seventeen villages, there are another fifty-four from the Ardèche, Drôme, Gard and Vaucluse *départements* whose wine may be called Côtes du Rhône-Villages, but which may not use their village name. These include Villedieu and Buisson, neither of which wished to be a named village originally but felt later that their wine was worthy of the higher status.

In order to be called Côtes du Rhône-Villages, a wine must do more than come from the specified villages; it must also satisfy stricter production requirements than Côtes du Rhône. Red 'Villages' wine must be at least 12.5 degrees alcohol (compared with 11 degrees for Côtes du Rhône), while white and rosé must be 12 degrees. In addition the yields must be less, to curb overproduction, and are restricted to 35 hectolitres per hectare, which is even less than for Hermitage and St-Joseph, where 40 is the permitted yield. The use of the Carignan grape is restricted to a maximum of 15 per cent.

Many of the villages making Côtes du Rhône-Villages will offer a Côtes du Rhône as well, which may form the larger part of their production. This is because the higher yields of 50 hectolitres per hectare are judged to outweigh considerably the slightly lower price fetched by Côtes du Rhône compared with 'Villages' wine. Some producers argue that the quality is hardly affected in spite of the higher yield and lower degree of alcohol; alcohol itself does not enhance quality – the way it is balanced with other constituents matters more. As a result the production

of Côtes du Rhône-Villages is still comparatively small, less than a tenth of that of Côtes du Rhône.

Most of the Côtes du Rhône-Villages wines are red, but a little white and rosé are made, not of any real commercial significance. Two of the villages are Beaumes-de-Venise and Rasteau, which also produce a dessert wine, known as *Vin Doux Naturel*. Each of these merits a separate appellation and have been described earlier.

Unlike Côtes du Rhône, which is often a blend of wines from all over the region, a Côtes du Rhône-Villages is more likely to retain some characteristics of its individual location. The Vaucluse-based villages tend to produce the fullest, most concentrated wines, while those from the Gard are lighter and more delicate. The Drôme villages are less well known than those in the Vaucluse, and each one's production is dominated by the cooperatives. Each village is reviewed below, in alphabetical order.

BEAUMES-DE-VENISE

Beaumes-de-Venise is a lovely, quiet old village, dating from the 8th century, situated in the foothills of the Vaucluse mountains close to the Dentelles de Montmirail. It is best known for the Muscat dessert wine, but some red wine is produced under the Côtes du Rhône-Villages appellation. Before the Muscat wine became popular in the UK towards the end of the 1970s, more red wine than Muscat was shipped from Beaumes-de-Venise. The balance has now shifted dramatically in the opposite direction.

CAIRANNE

This village is situated about 17 kilometres/10 miles north-east of Orange, on the road between Bollène and Carpentras, although it is relatively peaceful. Cairanne is on the top of gently rising land above the gradually undulating vineyard slopes that lie around it. At the highest point in the village is a fourteenth-century tower of the Knights Templar, which provides an excellent view over the whole district. The tower also houses an art gallery and wine museum.

The vineyards surrounding Cairanne fall into two groups: those on the plateau north of the village enjoy a clayey soil, while those on the barer countryside to the south are planted on poor, stony, gravelly ground which gives wines that are more deeply coloured, alcoholic and tannic than the elegant, rounded ones from the north. Red Cairanne is one of the more powerful Côtes du Rhône-Villages wines, with some of the qualities of a Châteauneuf-du-Pape, although it will not last as long – less than eight years.

Three-quarters of the wines from Cairanne are red; most of the rest is rosé and a little white is also made. The cooperative dominates the production at Cairanne, though some notable domaines also exist. One up and coming wine is from the Château de Cairanne, just outside the village itself.

CHUSCLAN

Chusclan is one of the three villages in the Gard *département*. It is best known for its rosé wines although larger quantities of red are produced, together with a little white. Chusclan wines come from an area of 560 hectares/1384 acres which extend also over the communes of Orsan, Codolet and St-Étienne-des-Sorts, each of which has its own *cave coopérative*. The cooperative at Chusclan itself makes all the wine grown in the actual commune of Chusclan. Its wines are medium-bodied, clean and fruity with a supple roundness.

LAUDUN

Laudun is also situated in the Gard, just a couple of miles south of Chusclan. These vineyards are among the oldest in the Gard, dating back to at least 300 BC, according to old amphorae found in the region. Two other communes come under the Laudun banner: St Victor la Coste and Tresques. North of the village of Laudun itself is a plain, known as Le Plateau du Camp de César, where many of the vineyards are planted; others are planted on the hillsides near the village and around the plateau cliff.

Laudun makes a red wine to rival that of Chusclan, and rather a good white from Clairette and Roussanne varieties. The wines are made at three *caves coopératives* and by three growers, of which the best known is Domaine Pelaquié.

RASTEAU

This village, like Beaumes-de-Venise, is better known for its *Vin Doux Naturel* (see page 25), though it makes all three colours of wine under the Côtes du Rhône-Villages appellation. Rasteau is situated about 20 kilometres/12 miles north-east of Orange, within a few miles each of Cairanne and Roaix, and the town of Vaison-la-Romaine. Red wine, made predominantly from Grenache (also used for the *Vin Doux Naturel*), forms the majority of the Villages wines. Four-fifths of the wine comes from the cooperative, Les Caves des Vignerons, while there are also a number of private growers. The wines are robust with plenty of fruit and backbone; the rosés are clean and lively.

ROAIX

Just a short distance north-east of Rasteau is the medieval village of Roaix, beside the Ouvèze river. The vineyards are planted on heavy soil with stones. The *Cave Coopérative de Roaix–Séguret* makes virtually all the wine here, three-quarters of which is red and the rest rosé. The wines are not considered among the best of the appellation, but the town is still worth visiting for its picturesque scenery.

ROCHEGUDE

Rochegude is situated south-east of Bollène near the villages of St Cécile-les-Vignes and Suze-la-Rousse, which has its own '*Université de Vin*', a wine museum and venue for courses on wine. Rochegude has its own château, dominating the village, which is now a luxury hotel whose restaurant also boasts one Michelin star. The vineyards are located on a plain, and are mainly planted with Grenache and Cinsault. Red wine is the principal produce here; solid, fruit-filled wines with a full bouquet and supple roundness. Some ordinary rosé and white wines are also made, but only under the lesser Côtes du Rhône appellation.

ROUSSET-LES-VIGNES AND ST-PANTALÉON-LES-VIGNES

Rousset-les-Vignes and St-Pantaléon-les-Vignes are neighbouring villages north-east of Valréas; they are the northernmost villages in the Côtes du Rhône-Villages appellation, and share a cooperative, the sole producer here. They are set amid striking scenery; the foothills of the Alps, south of Die, form a severe backdrop to the villages. The vineyards are planted in fertile, green land watered by mountain streams. The vines are on flat clay and limestone ground, with some on more gravelly slopes.

The wine is mostly red, with a heady 13 degrees alcohol, while only a little rosé and white of little consequence is made.

SABLET

Sablet is a small village just a mile or so south-west of Séguret; it is a Romanesque fortified village with similar spectacular views to those enjoyed from Séguret. Even though it was not promoted to Côtes du Rhône-Villages status until 1974, nevertheless the village thrives on its wine production. The name derives from the sandy soil in the vineyards surrounding the village, which give a light, delicate wine, most of which comes from *Le Gravillas Coopérative*. Most of Sablet's wine is red and rosé, with a little white; there are a number of private domaines

*Sablet is built on sandy soil on a small hill above the Vaucluse plain.
Its Roman church can be seen from approach roads several miles away.*

as well as the cooperative. One of Sablet's main claims to fame is that a grafting machine was invented here.

ST-GERVAIS

St-Gervais is (alphabetically speaking) the third village under the appellation from the Gard, and possibly the best thought-of, mainly because of the splendid Domaine Ste-Anne, which makes a red with a good proportion of the classy Mourvèdre and Syrah, but more unusually a delicious white wine from the Viognier grape, which does not normally stray outside Condrieu and Château Grillet. The volume production from this village comes largely from the cooperative, which has 158 members from a village population of only 500 or so. The cooperative wine is made on largely traditional lines and is probably less well known than that of Laudun or, more particularly, Chusclan.

ST-MAURICE-SUR-EYGUES

St-Maurice-sur-Eygues is a tiny village, comprising little more than the crossroads between the Bollène Nyons road and the junction towards Vaison. As with several other villages, the production of wine is almost entirely dominated by the local cooperative, the *Cave des Coteaux de St-Maurice-sur-Eygues*. The village takes its name from the Eygues river (which becomes the Aigues nearer the Rhône). Slopes rising up from the river form the sites for the vineyards, which are mainly planted with Grenache. Red wine forms the bulk of the production.

SÉGURET

Séguret joins forces with Roaix from the point of view of wine production. As a village, however, it deserves a visit in its own right and, time permitting, a meal in the picturesque La Table du Comtat overlooking the Plan de Dieu plain below.

VACQUEYRAS

Vacqueyras is probably one of the best known and highest quality Côtes du Rhône-Villages wines under this appellation. It is situated just south of Gigondas, on the D8 between Bollène and Carpentras.

Much of the red wine aspires to a status above that expected for the appellation – I would not be surprised to see this village being upgraded in status soon, in the manner of Gigondas: big, black-coloured, smoky, peppery wine that sometimes resembles wines from the North; Paul Jaboulet Aîné's Vacqueyras is one such wine. It tastes of Syrah yet is predominantly from the Grenache grape. Other producers, such as at the Clos des Cazaux, do use a large quantity of Syrah. The *Cave Coopérative* at Vacqueyras also produces sound, robust wine: it is called Le Troubadour after Vacqueyras' famous troubadour, and village idiot, Raimbaud. Roger Combe also makes fine, deep coloured, concentrated Vacqueyras (as well as Gigondas) which is worth seeking out.

The stony soil near Vacqueyras gives the wines their fruit and concentration. Most of the village's production is red; the small amounts of white and rosé produced do not reach anything approaching the same standard.

VALRÉAS

Valréas sits on a hill in an isolated part of the Vaucluse, protected on all sides by a ring of hills separating this 'island' from the surrounding Drôme *département*. Valréas forms the centre of 200 square kilometres/77 sq. miles known as the Enclave des Papes: this old papal enclave comprises the village of Valréas, Grillon, Visan and Richerenches.

Valréas has a twelfth-century Roman church and an eighteenth-century château at the top; traffic is mostly confined to the small ring road surrounding the old part of the town. The vineyards lie on the virtually flat areas surrounding the hill on a variety of different terrains: pebbles here, clay and limestone there. The area can be very bleak in winter, as the mistral wind can be very chilly indeed as it blows unhindered across the vineyards.

Valréas is famous for three products: wine, cardboard boxes and truffles (from the nearby woods). The wine is mainly red, with a little rosé, and is robust, peppery and has plenty of fruit, maturing relatively early. A number of growers produce their own wine at Valréas, while others belong to the *Cave Coopérative, La Gaillarde*. There is also a bottling plant just outside the town, the Cellier de l'Enclave des Papes, which bottles cooperative and private producers' wines.

VINSOBRES

The sober wine: what a splendidly paradoxical name! Compared with Valréas, Vinsobres, 15 kilometres/9 miles to the south-east, is rather small and quiet. It lies just outside the Enclave des Papes, near Nyons in the Drôme, and close to the river Eygues. The vineyards lie either side of the river.

Vinsobres wine production is dominated by two cooperatives: the *Vinsobraise*, where wine is largely made, and the *Cave du Prieuré*, which specializes in ageing and selling (rather than making) the wine. This is often aged in wood for long periods, rather a gamble for the lightish Vinsobres wine in all but the better vintages. Vinsobres also boasts six good domaines.

At its best Vinsobres can be complex, with smoky, berry fruit and peppery, herby overtones. Sadly, little is sold under the village name but much is declassified as Côtes du Rhône as up to 50 hectolitres per hectare can be made compared with 35 for Côtes du Rhône-Villages and the two wines sell at not dissimilar prices. At Vacqueyras, the same reasons have also been advanced by some producers against applying for full AC status.

CÔTES DU RHÔNE-VILLAGES		
Gard	**Drôme**	**Vaucluse**
Chusclan	Rochegude	Beaumes-de-Venise
Laudun	Rousset-les-Vignes	Cairanne
St-Gervais	St-Maurice-sur-Eygues	Rasteau
	St-Pantaléon-les-Vignes	Roaix
	Vinsobres	Sablet
		Séguret
		Vacqueyras
		Valréas
		Visan

VISAN

Visan is the second village besides Valréas with the right to Côtes du Rhône-Villages status inside the Enclave des Papes. It has plenty of quaint medieval charm, and the old part of the town also stands on a little hill. For a long time production of Visan wine centred almost entirely on the *Coteaux de Visan* cooperative, which makes the bulk of the wine, but recently two private domaines, Domaine de Cantharide and Clos du Père Clément, have been established, each making high quality red Visan Villages. The Cantharide wine has plenty of Syrah and Mourvèdre; indeed the village's plantations as a whole are seeing an increase in the proportion of Syrah, mainly at the expense of Grenache.

CÔTES DU RHÔNE

The basic Côtes du Rhône wines form the foundation of the whole region's wines, comprising over 80 per cent of the total volume produced. The vast majority of these wines are red, but a little rosé and white wine is also produced, though little, of the rosé in particular, is exported.

The quality of generic Côtes du Rhône is mostly reliable though differing in style. While a few of the wines are mediocre or simply badly made, many will be of satisfyingly good, consistent quality, and others bearing this simple appellation can be splendid with longer keeping potential. These latter are usually single domaine wines, rather than generic blends, as

Towering above the village of Suze la Rousse is its own university,
but with only a limited curriculum – all the courses are about wine!

the producer then has the opportunity to stamp his individual style on the wine. Seventy per cent of Côtes du Rhône is, however, made by the cooperatives.

The *appellation contrôlée* laws governing the production of Côtes du Rhône are comparatively generous. Minimum alcohol levels need only be 11 degrees for all wines (although many producers have no difficulty in producing a 12 degrees wine in all but the poorest years). The yield must not exceed 50 hectolitres per hectare and there are no restrictions on which grape varieties may be planted, though the Carignan must not exceed 30 per cent of the blends. In general, for red wines, the base is of Grenache, with Syrah, Mourvèdre and Cinsault being used to add more flavour and character. The huge variety of styles of red Côtes du Rhône that are available stems not only from the large number of possible combinations of grape variety and differing soils and aspects of the vineyards, but also because of the different vinification methods. Although it is hard to generalize on this matter, many of the cooperatives use a wine made by *macération carbonique* as the basis of their blend to give colour and suppleness, with some traditionally fermented wine to add backbone and tannin. The wine should be supple, medium-bodied and easy to drink, without too much tannin or astringence. A well-made cooperative wine should be drinkable within a year of the harvest and could be expected to last until it is five years old at least.

The domaine wines are made in smaller quantities than cooperative ones. Few make enough to justify exporting abroad, though Château Malijay, for example, is huge: over 180 hectares/445 acres in size. There must be hundreds of individual estates all over the region. Some of the better estate wines, such as Cru de Coudelet (made in Châteauneuf-du-Pape by the Perrin family, who also own Château de Beaucastel), will contain a significant proportion of Syrah and Mourvèdre, in this case 20 per cent and 30 per cent respectively, to make a deeper coloured, more concentrated tannic wine, which keeps longer than generic Côtes du Rhône. Château de Fonsalette,

under the same ownership as Château Rayas in Châteauneuf-du-Pape, at Lagarde Paséol make two superb wines. One is on a par with Châteauneuf-du-Pape and their Cuvée de Syrah is like a Hermitage.

Of the domaines, obviously some will be better than others; your own opinion of each wine will depend on what style of wine you happen to prefer.

All *négociants* in the whole of the Rhône valley will naturally offer a Côtes du Rhône, as may some from the Midi, Provence or Burgundy. In general, the *négociant*'s wine may be expected to follow their house style; if you like their other wines, you will probably also enjoy their Côtes du Rhône.

Generic Côtes du Rhône (from whatever provenance) should be medium to deep crimson-coloured, very fruity and peppery when young, maturing quickly to give a smoky, vegetal, herby aroma and fruit flavour. The lesser wines may be light and resemble strawberry jam on the nose, but are infinitely preferable to the disgusting, baked, oxidized wines, thin yet harsh, that still sometimes creep on to the market. Try before you buy if you can.

White Côtes du Rhône is increasing in popularity in Britain, probably because the quality has improved considerably in recent years. Fermentation under controlled conditions can produce fresh wines from a number of different grape varieties, including Marsanne, Roussanne, Clairette, Bourboulenc, Picpoul, Grenache blanc and Ugni blanc. The better wines are pale in colour, medium-bodied, dry with refreshing fruitiness and a crisp finish. Less-well-made wines have a tendency to be rather heavy and ill-balanced.

Rosé wine is practically never exported and is mostly consumed within the region. It is made using a similar mix of grapes as for red wines, but fermented with the skins present for only a day. They are more reliable in quality than an unknown white, and also need to be drunk very young. In the region rosé is often served as an aperitif mixed with a little *crème de myrtilles*, known as a Myro, the Rhône valley's answer to the Burgundian Kir.

CÔTES DU RHÔNE		
Top Producers	**Recommended Producers**	**Recommended *Négociants***
Château de Fonsalette	Château Malijay	Paul Jaboulet Aîné
Cru du Coudelet	La Vieille Ferme	E. Guigal
	St-Estève	Caves St-Pierre
	Château de Domazan	
	Château du Grand Moulas	
	Domaine des Treilles	

LESSER APPELLATIONS

In recent years many previously unheard of regions have started to produce good wine. Not all of these have yet achieved *appellation contrôlée* status, but they are worth watching for in the future.

COTEAUX DU TRICASTIN

This relatively new appellation has risen considerably in the ranks in recent years. The Rhône valley's fastest growing viticultural region, Coteaux du Tricastin was not even recognized as VDQS status until 1964, but achieved *appellation contrôlée* just ten years later. The area lies east of the river between Montélimar and Bollène. It covers eight communes centred round Les Granges Gontardes: La Baume de Transit, Roussons, Allan, Malataverne, Valaurie, Donzère and Grignan (bordering on Valréas).

The unexpected name of this region comes not from any particular village or site but from a tribe of warriors called the Tricastini, who fought the Romans and lost as Gaul fell to the invaders. As well as wine, the area is famous for truffles from the woods near Valréas. The unwooded parts of the Coteaux du Tricastin are barren and exposed to the full force of the wind, and can be very bleak and cold in winter. In autumn the ripening grapes are helped along by heat-retaining big, creamy white stones similar to the pebbles of Châteauneuf-du-Pape.

Vine varieties that are planted include the Grenache, predominantly, Cinsault, Syrah, Mourvèdre and Carignan, but with a small quantity of white grapes, as 95 per cent of the wine made here is red. The red is lighter than its good colour and powerful bouquet would suggest; the wines are fresh and supple and mature rapidly. They lack the power or concentration of a big Châteauneuf-du-Pape or Gigondas but make their impression with their intense raspberry aromas and flavour. The wines are delicious after two years, and will keep until they are four to five years old.

The area comprises numerous domaines and a *cave coopérative* in the village of Richerenches. One of the top domaines in recent years has been Domaine de la Tour d'Elyssas, whose future is now sadly in jeopardy following financial difficulties in the early 1980s and the death of the owner, Pierre Labeye, in 1987. The domaine boasts an enormous vinification tower, 15 metres/50ft high, built in the mid-1960s. Once vats have been filled, the must passes through the system by gravity; no pumping is necessary. The exposure of the vats to the air ensures that they are cooled naturally by the wind. Only a very few such towers exist; there are no others in the Rhône valley.

CÔTES DU VIVARAIS

Unlike Coteaux du Tricastin, the Côtes du Vivarais is not yet an *appellation contrôlée* area, just VDQS, though promotion is soon awaited. The vineyards are on the west bank of the Rhône, opposite Tricastin, between the towns of Viviers and Pont St Esprit in the beautiful, unspoilt Ardèche *département*, famed for its gorges, caves and grottoes, and fast streams containing delicious freshwater fish.

The Vivarais is as yet little known, making solid, fruity, good value reds and rather dull white and rosé, though these are happily in the minority. The grapes planted on this district's limestone soil are the standard selection: Grenache, Syrah, Mourvèdre, Cinsault and the white Picpoul. Seven hundred and thirty hectares/1800 acres of a potential 8000 hectares are currently under vines so the area could expand considerably in the future.

The wines are made by both traditional and *macération carbonique* methods according to the individual producers. Fermentations tend to be short, and the wine is bottled early, as Vivarais wines do not have the potential to be very concentrated or long-lived. Instead they tend towards being reliable, fruity and quaffable; good commercial qualities to have. They are good served chilled, as well as at room temperature.

A number of villages in the region have a *cave coopérative*, of which those at Orgnac, Ruoms and St-Montan are considered the best. There are few good private domaines, the best of which is Domaine de Belvezet; wines in this category should increase as the area gains fame and fortune.

COTEAUX DU TRICASTIN
Recommended Producers
Domaine de la Tour d'Elyssas Domaine de Grangeneuve Château des Estubiers

CÔTES DU VIVARAIS	
Recommended Producers	
M. Brunel (Domaine de Belvezet)	Mme. Gallety (Domaine Gallety)
M. Dupré (Domaine de Vigier)	Cave Coopérative de St-Montan

CÔTES DU VENTOUX

Not so long ago, the Mont Ventoux was better known in France for bicycle races than growing vines. Since 1974, however, the region has been firmly established as an *appellation contrôlée*, mostly for red wines, with a little white and rosé. The countryside is wild and unspoilt, with the dramatic silhouette of the mountain rising in the background. The 8000 hectares (almost 20000 acres) of vineyards currently planted all lie on the southern side of the foot of the mountain. The designated area comprises village communities in two rows, separated by a sweeping valley containing cherry orchards and vines of Muscat table grapes as well as wine vines. The vineyard area extends from Malaucène in the north to Pernes les Fontaines and Apt, south of Carpentras, in the south.

Some vineyards are planted at an altitude of over 400 metres/1400ft; this is approaching the maximum height at which viticulture can be successfully achieved. Grapes in these parts will ripen later than their counterparts in the valley and make lighter but perhaps more elegant wine. This factor and the different soil structure from the nearby Côtes du Rhône vineyards both contribute to the lighter, more quaffable qualities of the Ventoux wines, though similar grape varieties are planted.

Many wines are made *en café*, that is with a very short fermentation and a short period in vat before being bottled early. Such wines are light in colour, depth and body and will age quickly. A few producers, however, give their wines longer maceration in order to extract more colour, tannin and staying power from the grapes. Jean-Pierre Perrin of La Vieille Ferme makes a wine that is ready to drink quite early, but is full-bodied and robust.

The area is dominated by the cooperatives, who are supplied by a large proportion of the 4000 growers in the region, though there are a handful of private growers of note.

CÔTES DU VENTOUX	
Recommended Producers	
M. Perrin (La Vieille Ferme)	M. Quiot (Domaine Vieux Lazaret)
M. Swan (Domaine des Anges)	M. Rey (Domaine St-Sauveur)

CLAIRETTE DE DIE

In Pliny's time, there stood a town called Dea Augusta on the river Drôme. Today is it known as Die, the home of a sparkling wine that claims to be even older than champagne, dating back to AD 77.

Die is situated in mountainous countryside in the first foothills of the Alps, south of the Vercors Regional Park, surrounded by vines and walnut trees. Both still and sparkling wines are made here; while the former is often rather dull and flavourless, the latter can be of great interest. The *brut* sparkling wine is made entirely from the Clairette grape, from which it takes its name, but the Clairette de Die *Tradition* (in *brut* or *demi-sec* styles) is half to three-quarters comprised of the spicy, scented Muscat variety. The inclusion of this noble variety gives the *Tradition* wine a big advantage over the *Brut* and still wines.

Muscat is difficult to grow well in most circumstances but it thrives on the rocky ground near the mountains. Otherwise the soil is of clay and limestone, better suited to the hardier Clairette.

Vintage time is quite late, between October and November each year. The *Brut* wines are made according to the *méthode champenoise*, while the *Tradition* is made slightly differently (see page 24), usually without a vintage date, though in exceptional years a vintage *cuvée* may be made. The *Brut* is light, pleasing but fairly neutral in style, while the *Tradition* wine is darker in colour and considerably more perfumed and aromatic. The sparkling wine has a life span of three years only; it is not a wine to keep.

The main source of Clairette de Die is the *Union des Producteurs* in Die itself, though there are some noteworthy growers as well.

CLAIRETTE DE DIE	
Recommended Producers	
Union des Producteurs de Die	M. Archard-Vincent
	Buffardel Frères
M. Archard	M. Vincent

*Unlike the mountainous terrain in the northern Rhône, the Vaucluse country is gently undulating.
Rows of cypress trees are frequently planted alongside the vineyards to shield them from
the mistral wind. Also for this reason, the vines are trained close to the ground.*

I N D E X

ACKNOWLEDGEMENTS

Editor: Isobel Greenham
Art Editor and Designer: Bob Gordon
Picture Research: Julia Pashley

Map illustrations: Andrew Farmer
Grape illustrations: Nicki Kemball

The Publishers would like to thank the following photographers and organisations for their kind permission to reproduce their photographs:
Michael Busselle 1, 24-5, 46-7, 65, 73; Cuisine et Vins De France 17, 59, 67; Patrick Eagar 2-3, 8-9, 36-7, 41, 42, 44, 50, 51, 52-3; Explorer/F Jalain 48, 63, 68, 71, 73, 77; Susan Griggs Agency/C W Friend 58/9; The Photographers Library/Michael Busselle 15; Zefa Picture Library 61.